# GUIDE TO NORSE PAGANISM

A COMPREHENSIVE GUIDE EXPLORING
NORSE PAGAN HISTORY & CULTURE, VIKINGS,
MYTHS AND LEGENDS OF THE NORSE GODS &
GODDESSES, CREATION OF THE UNIVERSE,
RUNES, RITUALS, SYMBOLS, AND DIVINATION.

EMMA KARLSSON

# COPYRIGHT

# CONTENTS

# FREE GIFT JUST FOR YOU!!!

## 2023 NORSE GOD & GODDESSES CALENDAR

http://bit.ly/3iEs12l

# INTRODUCTION

A white-bearded figure walks through a green field against a splendid backdrop of snow-covered mountains. Donning a weathered robe and a long, pointed hat and wielding an adorned cane that, upon closer look, reveals a concealed spear, this mystical figure wanders with poise, and as he walks, you see that two wolves match his gait at his heels. Above him, two ravens fly close by, cawing, crooning, keeping a weather eye on the horizon.

Above him, the sky broods with storm clouds and the deep roar of thunder. Below him, the seas send tide after tide to clash against the jagged rocks on the Scandinavian cliffside.

You do not take long to realize that you are in a state of trance. This is a vision. You see the wanderer from far across the fjord as he traverses across the countryside.

It is only when he turns in your direction, and his piercing blue eye gazes into your soul do you realize something.

It is no coincidence that you are here.

The roots of the Yggdrasil run deep, binding the world together and beckoning seekers from far and wide. I will say it again. It is no coincidence that you are here. If it is dissent from modern organized religion that has turned your heart away from the fulfillment that faith can offer, you are in the right place. If you seek deific mysteries passed through the ages, mysteries that speak of godly figures that once walked this realm, mysteries that painted this common world of ours into a place of wonder and fantasy, you are in the right place.

If you seek to break free of the tethers that have confined your belief to monotony, if you yearn to unleash the acolyte within, you are in the right place. Here we ditch conforming norms and wear the pagan garb, divining deeper meaning in runes and fostering harmony with arcane lore that will help you reveal the truth about yourself.

Before we delve into the intricacies of this beautiful creed, I want to welcome all, wherever it is that you may have come from, whatever your background is.

It may be that:

## Modern Renditions in Pop-Culture Piqued Your Interest

You have seen the resurgence of Nordic lore in recent pop culture, from *Marvel's* adaptation of *Thor* to *Assassin's Creed's* portrayal of Vikings. If you are more of a book-worm like me, you might have come across modern inter-pretations of the Nordic pantheon of deities in works of literature such as *American Gods* by the venerable Neil Gaiman. That same author who gave us the beloved world of Sandman also wrote a concise history of Norse gods in his book, *Norse Mythology*, faithfully retelling ancient tales to a new audience. History Channel's critically acclaimed TV show *Vikings* conjures a sense of grandeur as it tells the tale of Ragnar Lothbrok. Young adult authors like Rick Riordan are infusing their works with Norse mythology. Video games franchises such as *God of War* have made use of Norse mythology's rich culture and have placed their game setting within locations such as Midgard. Many notable works of fiction, such as *Lord of The Rings*, have taken a huge amount of inspiration from Norse mythology.

## Present-Day Religions Have Failed To Inspire You

You have explored modern interpretations of Abrahamic religions such as Christianity, Judaism, and Islam and have felt disconcerted by their organized and restrictive nature. This disconcertment has led you to explore other creeds and faiths wherein you feel more in tune with the world around you, are more of an active participant in religious activities, and feel accomplished after having performed your rites. The sense of freedom that Norse paganism offers will come as a welcome change of pace, reorienting your entire worldview.

## You Seek A Deeper, More Meaningful Existence

The primal nature of Norse mythology speaks to you. Many of us feel tied into the cyclical nature of our daily lives, unable to escape from the dystopic web that late-stage capitalism, organized religion devoid of spirituality, and the debilitating blandness of our routines have woven around us. I'm talking about a life that's impeded by subpar, processed food that doesn't nurture, an unending barrage of entertainment thrown in our faces in the form of infinitely scrollable social media feeds, binge-able episodes of seasons after seasons of media meant to sedate us, and a listless existence centered around keeping oneself trapped in a loop of earning and spending money. In the face of all this, the old Norse religion comes bearing liberty, letting you harness your primal self and allowing you to unlock your spiritual, physical, material, and emotional potential.

## Your Quest for Knowledge Has Left You With Many Questions

As with any topic that possesses a substantial history, ties to a certain region, and a culture that dates back thousands of years, Norse Paganism, encompassing all its beliefs and practices, is a deep subject that requires an equally deep understanding of the nuances of its beliefs, evolution, and history.

- You might be wondering what Norse Paganism is, who its followers were, and how is it different from other religions.
- Have you wondered how many gods there are in the Norse pantheon? What their powers are, what traits do they carry, and what elements do they have control over?
- Is there a form of worship that allows you to harness the spirituality associated with those gods?
- How do I become a Norse Pagan?
- What do Norse Pagans believe in?
- What are the different types of religious practices I can follow as a Pagan?

- What benefit—spiritual or material—do I stand to gain from following this religion?

If these are some of the questions that you have pondered over, I have glad tidings for you. First off, you are a kindred spirit, and I welcome you in this quest to uncover ancient truths and wisdom. Secondly, you are in the right place. Throughout this book, I will help answer all the questions that you might have, provide you with a direction, and instill awe for the wonders that Norse Paganism has to offer.

**What Exactly Is Norse Paganism?**

Norse Paganism encompassed the beliefs, customs, practices, and world views that the Northern European civilizations followed before Christianity pervaded throughout the region.

Modern-day Norse Paganism is an adaptation of the spiritual beliefs and practices of the Norse folk. The Norse were a diverse group of people in terms of their crafts, occupations, lifestyle choices, and values. For example, the term Vikings, although used synonymously with Norse people, was just one of the many roles that the Norse people had adapted. Despite their different roles, the Norse folk shared a common belief system which gave rise to their religious practices.

**Norse Paganism differs from other religions because it is:**

- Polytheistic
- Orthopraxical
- Pluralist

- Decentralized
- Animistic
- Immanent

Now, what does that mean?

**Polytheistic**

While Abrahamic religions such as Christianity and Islam believe in one god, Norse Paganism is polytheistic. It believes in multiple gods. The most prominent deities in the Norse pantheon include Odin, Thor, Loki, Balder, Frigg, Heimdall, and Tyr. Each god bore specific characteristics associated with the domain they held power over. Thor, for example, was the god of thunder and therefore harnessed the powers of thunder using his weapon, Mjölnir.

Since the religion was decentralized, different gods had different levels of devotion in different places at different times. A fishing hamlet by the sea might have venerated Njord, the god of the wind and the sea and all the riches it contained, while at the same time, a mountain village might have worshipped Ullr and Skaði, the deities associated with winter.

Its polytheistic nature allowed quite a bit of liberty in terms of choosing which deity to venerate.

**Orthopraxical**

When it comes to religious thought, there exist two main schools—orthodoxy and orthopraxy. Orthodoxy means "the right belief," whereas Orthopraxy means "the right practice." While some religions take a polarized approach to these schools of thought, employing one instead of the other, some religions utilize both aspects. However, Norse Paganism believes in orthopraxy.

Orthopraxical religions prioritize and incentivize experience, the integrity of one's practice, the creation and continuation of one's lineage, and one's legacy. In sheer contrast, orthodox religions prioritize adherence to dogmas, doctrines, creeds, and faith above action.

Orthopraxy also means what's the right action for a certain individual rather than what's been deemed right for them according to some religious authority.

**Pluralist**

All religions have philosophies rooted in them, which serve as the building blocks of the faith and its practices. The philosophy behind doing virtuous acts is that one will be granted rewards in the afterlife. Such philosophy can also serve as the foundation of religious morality. This philosophy can also be used as a device to spiritually relate one thing to another.

Norse Paganism follows a pluralistic philosophy. Pluralism, in contrast to the dualist and monist philosophies, believes that everything contains profound multitudes, that even the most ordinary of things have different principles, and that the truth behind things is not absolute. Rather, it takes multiple forms and is even bound to shift.

The plurality of Norse Paganism creates a nuanced worldview where things, entities, people, and forces are viewed as more than just good or evil. Pluralists believe that everything is multifaceted, possessing both a light side and a darker side, and it is within the balance of both sides that one can look at a picture clearly and decipher its meaning.

Unlike Norse Paganism, Christianity, Judaism, and Islam have a dualist philosophy, where the categorization of good and evil is used to describe things. Sin and virtue, heaven and hell, and angels and demons are just some dualist aspects of these religions.

Some branches of Sufism and Pantheism can be considered monist beliefs, where everything is just an expression of the Universe or its Creator. Monists believe in the Source and believe that all things come from a place of singular origin.

**Decentralized**

Christianity's centralized source of instruction comes from the Bible. With Judaism, it's the Torah. In Islam, Muslims adhere to the guidelines as noted in the Quran and Hadith. This makes these religions centralized, with a singular source serving as the foundation of ideologies, laws, and practices.

Norse Paganism is a decentralized religion with no singular authority or ideology behind the religion. There aren't any central holy books, religious figures, scriptures, doctrines, or dogmas that a Norse Pagan has to adhere to.

Given that most religions have a demanding nature wherein they require a commitment of time and resources, selecting authorities, delegating orthodox beliefs, and behavioral codes that include rules of dress, diet, and sexual practices, it might come as a shock to people that Paganism, unlike its counterparts, does not carry such a rigorous eligibility criterion, thanks to its decentralized nature.

An argument can be made for the authenticity of Norse Paganism because of its decentralized nature. Since there's not one singular source but many, many of those sources corroborate each other, validating each other's beliefs, thus bringing credibility to the religion's beliefs because its multiple sources substantiate the same thing.

The decentralized nature of Norse mythos and Paganism meant that it grew organically throughout a community via local customs and oral narration of traditions.

The Prose and Poetic Edda, while considered exhaustive texts with much lore and mythology, are not deemed religious scriptures.

### Animistic

Animism is a belief that recognizes that all objects, creatures, and places possess a spiritual essence. From rocks to rivers, plants to planets, everything—even words—is considered animated or alive. When you view things from an animistic perspective, you understand that everything, from the minutest of objects to the largest of beings, plays an integral role in the ecosystem that it exists in.

The existence of animism in Norse Paganism eliminates the distinction between holy and unholy, sacred and cursed. There's no concept of sinning in Norse Paganism. Your actions in the world are attributed to your existence rather than serve as a metric for some reward.

By assigning a spirit to every object and creature, animism opens the doors to near-infinite reserves of spirituality, giving birth to special rituals that can let you communicate with the spirits of the departed or form a bond with a deity by venerating them directly.

**Immanent**

Faith can be considered transcendent or immanent. Most faiths fall in either of these categories, although sometimes, some can have elements from both.

Transcendent faiths focus on *transcending* to a reality beyond our current one. The purpose of these faiths is to align your actions with a given set of instructions to fulfill the criteria to attain a desirable afterlife. In Christianity, your life choices will serve to bring you closer to God or drive you away from Him, determining whether you'll go to heaven or hell.

Immanent faiths, instead, focus on the actualization and fulfillment of your present life and the relationship that you have with the people and the world around you. Immanent faiths seek to improve the quality of your immediate reality.

Norse Paganism prides itself in being a religion that improves upon your current life by equipping you with skills, beliefs, principles, and practices that will improve your relationship with those around you, both people and nature, and let you experience living in a more primal manner. Many Pagans believe that we will be rejoined with our ancestors after we die unless we choose something else, such as a warrior's death which will result in us attaining an afterlife in Valhalla. But there is no pressure to live your life in a certain way to attain a desirable afterlife, unlike in Judeo-Christian religions, where heaven has to be earned.

## What Will This Book Entail?

When I set out to write this book, I wanted to create something that would initiate a newcomer to Norse Paganism with the prerequisite knowledge that will help establish a clear understanding of Norse Mythology and Paganism in their mind and provide them with tangible and followable guidelines on how to align themselves with the teachings and principles of Norse Paganism.

To that effect, we are going to study the following topics:

1. How you can become a Norse Pagan
2. The rich history and culture of the Nordic people
3. The creation of the world according to Norse mythology, what the nine realms are, and what the world tree, Yggdrasil, is
4. The Norse calendar, holidays, festivals, and celebrations
5. The Gods and Goddesses of the Norse Pantheon
6. The Many Magical Creatures that populate the Norse mythos
7. The afterlife according to Norse mythology. Here we shall explore topics such as Valhalla and Ragnarök.
8. Discovering the magic and mysticism of runes
9. The rites of passage and rituals associated with the natural cycle of birth, growth, and death.
10. What it means to be a Norse Pagan in the modern world.

After going through the contents of this book, you will have a blueprint that will allow you to practice Paganism on your own or with a community of like-minded souls. The purpose of this book is more than just to inform. I want to instill the same awe of Norse mythology and paganism in you that runs in my veins. I want to open your eyes to the wonders of this ancient world and show you that magic still exists. I want to empower you to such a point that you can harness that magic yourself.

## A Little About Me

I'm Emma Karlsson. Ever since I could remember, the stories of the old gods and goddesses have been there by my side. Growing up in Kungsträdgården, Sweden, I was surrounded by Scandinavian heritage. For me, the tales of Loki were more than just stories told to me at bedtime; for me, they were accounts of what had happened long ago, in a land where frost giants dwelled and warred with the armies of Odin.

I used to dress up as Freya and would ride a makeshift chariot that I made by tying my cats to a cart. I'd spend days upon days dreaming about the gods and goddesses who inhabited a wondrous, enchanted world, perfusing it with their magic.

It was my love of Norse mythology and culture that helped me develop a robust working knowledge of my religion and its roots. Although I was raised Christian, I always felt disconnected from Christianity. This wasn't the religion of my ancestors. Why was I following it?

In an attempt to connect with my ancestors and form a mutually respectful and loving bond with nature, I became a follower of Asatru, one of the modern interpretations of Paganism. I have devoted much of my learning to reading runes and understanding what it means to be a follower of the Old Norse Paganism belief systems. I continue to develop my knowledge base to share with my readers around the world. I believe that the magic of the world around us is precious and plentiful enough for all of us to experience. I want to bring that magic to you and share my love and passion for Norse Paganism and culture with kindred spirits such as yourself.

So let us venture forth and immerse ourselves in a world of wonders. Welcome to the realm of Norse Mythology.

# CHAPTER 1
# THE FRAMEWORK FOR BEING A NORSE PAGAN

The world as we know it has been rendered monotonously uniform as a result of aggressive corporatization, capitalism, and cultural wars that span centuries and continents.

Whether you're standing at the center of Times Square on New Year's Eve or backpacking through India after college, there's always a McDonald's nearby. Grocery stores all over the world contain the same Coke, the same Froot Loops, and the same Axe Body Spray. This rapid homogenization has taken the magic out of life.

Multimedia companies have ensured that we're all watching the same TV shows and movies, regardless of our location. Streaming platforms have morphed what was otherwise an enjoyable activity reserved for the weekend or date nights into a FOMO machine where if you haven't watched episode number x of show number y, you're going to miss out on all the great conversations surrounding that show on social media, almost forcing you to watch it just so you don't feel left out.

We have deviated from our traditions. Where are the old ways that our ancestors once used to live and thrive by? Is there no place for spirituality in the 21st century? Why has this rat-race-natured modern living robbed us of the mystical fulfillment that comes with following a creed?

Surely, you must have also thought along those lines at some point in your life. Perhaps that served as a cross-roads, leading you here, imploring you to seek deeper meaning in life, uncovering the ancient ways, the old religions that our ancestors used to follow.

If so, congratulations. You are a seeker. And it would please you to know that you are sought just as much as you seek. The old gods still live among us today, keeping an eye on those who possess the prerequisite spark that can be ignited into a fire of passion, devotion, and otherworldly satisfaction. It may very well be that your intrigue has fascinated the gods, and they have—through the means they possess—paved the way for you to uncover the truth.

It is your intrigue and fascination that have brought you this far. Going further, you are going to have to do some research into what Norse mythology entails and what constitutes some of the practices of Norse Paganism. This homework is necessary, as it's going to set you apart from someone just curious about what it means to be a Norse Pagan and will start you on a journey to becoming one.

The framework for becoming a Norse Pagan includes the following steps:

**Learning the fundamentals.** This includes acquainting yourself with the history of Norse Paganism as well as the general mythology that encircles Norse beliefs. Once you learn what's out there, you will form an opinion about it. As it's a whole new dimension of belief, one that you aren't used to, it's going to take some time to wrap your head around more complex topics, such as the cyclical nature of time in Norse mythology. Here, you will learn that the gods and goddesses are not perfect beings without any flaws such as the Abrahamic god. The gods of the Norse pantheon are complex beings with anthropomorphic characteristics, flaws, strengths, emotions, and fully-developed personalities.

**Understanding the Deeds.** Paganism includes several practices such as Blót, Veneration, Rune Divination, Sumbel, and Norse Magic. Norse Magic includes practices such as Spadom, Galdrastafir, and Seiðr. Seiðr, for example, is associated with prophecy and manifestation. In modern-day, Seiðr is associated with spiritual work such as inducing trances, seeing visions, and astral projection. To become a Norse Pagan is to first understand the meaning of different practices and deeds and then integrate them into your daily life to attain your goals, whatever they may be—spiritual elevation, the manifestation of desires, emotional contentment, and so on.

**Doing one's homework.** First, we have to understand that Norse mythology and, subsequently Norse Paganism are very decentralized entities. Unlike modern religions that come from a singular source, you have to read from different sources and form a coherent narrative for yourself that allows you to make sense of Norse mythology and its practices. Norse Pagans rely on sources such as the Prose Edda and the Poetic Edda, which are collections of Nordic stories and poems. As you expand your knowledge base, you will come across books such as Íslendingabók and Landnámabók that provide further detail about Norse myth and the accounts of the settling of Norse Vikings in places such as Iceland in the 9th and 10th centuries.

**Taking part in celebrations, rites of passage, offerings, and rune magic.** Once you have learned the fundamentals, understood the meaning behind the deeds, and done your homework, you are ready to take part in the Norse celebrations that the Pagans celebrate throughout their calendar year. Yule, Ostara, and Midsummer are some of the celebrations that the Norse used to celebrate at different points in the calendar period. You might want to learn about the rites of passage associated with Norse mythology and implement them in your life. At this stage, you are ready to include offerings and rune magic into your daily life as well, allowing you to truly become a Norse Pagan.

### Who are the Norse Gods?

A good starting point for your research would be finding out about the gods and goddesses of Norse mythology. Norse Paganism is a polytheistic religion populated with many gods and goddesses with their own set of abilities, strengths, domains, and characteristics.

As Norse mythology was largely passed down orally for centuries, the exact number of gods is hard to ascertain. Snorri Sturluson, an Icelandic figure most well-noted for his poetry and contribution to Norse history, did write down the mythologies in the form of the Eddas and the Heimskringla, which gives us a basic understanding of the gods, among other things.

In Norse mythology, the gods governed as mentors, guides, allies, protectors, and beings worthy of worship. According to Norse lore, the gods, being polytheistic, are not all-powerful or limitless. Each of them has a certain domain that they have mastery over. Understanding which god rules over which domain will give you a better understanding of what their true forms are like.

Perhaps one of the redeeming features of the Norse gods is their imperfection. While in conventional religions, the image of a monotheistic god is associated with perfection and flawlessness, the Norse gods have a much more relatable and approachable nature *because* they are imperfect. It's not just within the physical traits that they are imperfect—such as missing body parts or bearing battle scars—but it's also within their actions that they are flawed.

Where modern religions associate holiness with infallibility, Norse mythology presents its gods as fallible beings capable of error. Rather than paint the gods in a negative light, their imperfections cast light on the aspects that they are the gods of. For example, Loki, the god of mischief, is by his nature a god who relishes in deception and cunning, providing insight into the workings of what mischief is and what its limits can be. Similarly, Thor, known for his temper and his brute strength, resonates with the powers and traits of thunder.

The Norse gods were split into two categories:

• The Æsir

• The Vanir

**The Æsir**

These are the gods associated with humanity in a societal context such as through law, war, conflict, and labor. Odin, Thor, and Loki are some very famous Æsir gods. Other Æsir gods include Baldr, Foresti, Ullr, Bragi, and Iðunn.

Take Odin, for example. He is probably one of the most complex gods in Norse mythology. He is known as the Many-Named God because of his attributes, titles, and honors. He was seen as a god of war and death, but he was so much more than that. He is synonymous with the quest for knowledge, taking extreme measures to attain his goal whether it's losing an eye or hanging upside down from the World Tree.

**The Vanir**

The Vanir are gods associated with humanity's connection to nature, such as in magic and fertility. Some famous Vanir include Frey, Freya, and Njord. The Vanir are inherently different from the Æsir as they offer an understanding of how man is connected to the world around him. The Vanir have a mystical element that implores a learner to seek a deeper understanding of his relationship with the biosphere he lives in.

Freya, one of the Vanir, is considered the goddess of femininity, passion, and wisdom. Freya is also adept in the art of seiðr, a magic that she even taught to Odin. Besides being wise, strong, and beautiful, Freya was also able to shapeshift into a hawk and a falcon using her feathered cloak. Her very image evokes respect for nature.

Freya, one of the Vanir, is considered the goddess of femininity, passion, and wisdom. Freya is also adept in the art of seiðr, a magic that she even taught to Odin. Besides being wise, strong, and beautiful, Freya was also able to shapeshift into a hawk and a falcon using her feathered cloak. Her very image evokes respect for nature.

## The Jötnar

The Jötnar are considered gods by some practitioners. They are the gods of the wilderness, associated with raw forces of nature such as those that exist in the depths of oceans or wildfires. The Jötnar are associated with the elemental forces of nature including nature (earth) itself. You may consider them gods of deeper wisdom. Ymir, Surtr, Jord, Aegir, and Ran are some of the Jötnar.

These three clans have had a very complicated history with each other, sometimes warring with each other and sometimes seen establishing friendly relationships with each other, even marrying from each other's clans. When it comes to these gods, things aren't exactly split into clear black and white—there's no distinct divide between what constitutes good and evil. Ask yourself this: Can thunder be evil? Does fertility possess the capacity to be a dark force? Can the sea be a malevolent entity?

Of course, then some gods exist beyond any category: Hel, Níðhöggr, Fenrir, and Jörmungandr are all magnificent gods who embody primordial forces that are much more powerful and vast than any of the other gods from the previously mentioned categories. Hel, for example, is the guardian of the dead, connected to the spirits of those who have passed. Jörmungandr is a giant serpent who circles all of Midgard, representing the limits of all that is known.

## What Is the Norse World?

All the gods and goddesses that I mentioned thrive in the Norse world, a realm that contains multitudes in terms of mysticism, lore, and locations. The Norse Pagan world contains four main realities:

1. The World Tree Yggdrasil
2. The cyclical nature of the universe, starting from its birth and ending in Ragnarök
3. The spirits that thrive all around us in the world
4. The web of fate that encompasses everything

These realities—or *truths*—shape the perception of the Norse world.

# Yggdrasil and the Nine Realms

The world tree is the spiritual backbone of the Norse world. This great ash tree has roots that spread in every direction, extending into the nine realms and digging deep into the world to take its water from three wells, the Urdarbrunner (the Well of Fate), the Hvergelmir (the Roaring Kettle), and the Mimisbrunnr (Mimir's Well). Each of these wells has a rich history of its own.

Mimir's Well, for example, is the source of wisdom and contains waters for which Odin sacrificed his eye.

Upon the Yggdrasil, rest the nine realms. You may consider these parallel dimensions ruled by their own laws and governments. There's a hierarchy to these realms based on their respective position on the Yggdrasil.

The top two realms of Asgard and Vanaheim are at the top of the Yggdrasil and are home to the Æsir and Vanir gods. The gods of these realms use the Bifrost to travel from their realms to other realms. The Bifrost is a rainbow bridge guarded by Heimdall, one of the gods.

Near to these two realms lies the realm Alfheim, home of the powerful spirits known as the Alfar.

Then, halfway down, is Midgard. Midgard is basically our land. The Middle Realm. It's the realm containing the earth. The great beast Jörmungandr encircles Midgard's outer limits. This serpent holds its tail in its mouth.

Near Midgard is the land of the Jötnar, Jötunheimr. On the other side of Jötunheimr is Nidavellir, the home of the dwarves.

At the base of the Yggdrasil, there are two realms opposite each other. These are the realms of fire and ice, Muspelheim and Niflheim, respectively.

The final realm on Yggdrasil's base is Helheim, the land where the dead reside. It is here that the souls of the departed rest eternally.

At the root of the Yggdrasil, there's a dragon named Níðhöggr, who keeps gnawing away at the roots of the tree. His hunger will never be sated.

Yggdrasil's iconic position as the nurturer and nourisher of all the worlds makes it one of the most important fixtures of Norse Mythology.

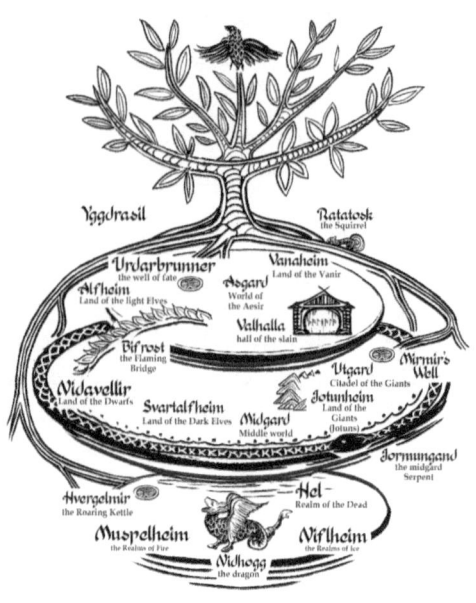

# The Cyclical Nature of Reality

The story of creation, as told in the Eddas, bears remarkable similarity to how the creation of the universe is detailed in modern science in the form of the Big Bang. In Norse mythology, there was nothing in the beginning except for a humongous void known as the Ginnungagap. This gap was surrounded by the fire of Muspelheim and the ice of Niflheim. And then, no one knows how long ago, a cosmic clash took place as both ice and flame met with vigor, causing an explosion the likes of which was never seen before.

This caused the great cow known as Auðumbla and the ferocious giant Ymir to come forth from the steam issuing from the explosion. While Ymir gave birth to the giants, the first of the Jötnar, from his body, the cow Auðumbla unearthed the first of the Æsir by licking away mist off the rocks. The first of the Æsir was Búri. Búri had children with a giant, including a son named Bor.

Bor then had three sons with a frost giant: Odin, Vili, and Ve.

Together, these brothers ended the age of the Great Giants and ushered in a new era.

Odin and his siblings slew Ymir after they couldn't take any more of their poverty, given that Ymir was hoarding Auðumbla's boons for himself. Ymir's body was used to craft existence as we know it.

Midgard was created after the gods decided upon the details through consulting with each other. The first humans began inhabiting Midgard.

And just as this creation took place, so too will cyclical destruction take place, known as Ragnarök. Foretold by the Nameless Seeress, Ragnarök is the end of the world in the aftermath of a great battle.

Heimdall shall sound his horn for the first and final time, summoning the gods and their kin to battle. A time of bitter cold known as Fimbulwinter will bring forth frost the likes of which has not been seen before. The great wolf Fenrir shall break free and wreak havoc. Jörmungandr will rise from the sea and cause the land to be flooded. Surtr shall gather an army of fire giants in Muspelheim.

The armies shall battle with each other. Surtr will fight Frey. Thor shall wrestle Jörmungandr and perish. Odin shall be devoured by Fenrir. A big hound called Garm shall come out and slay Tyr, the god of war and justice. Loki will arrive with his forces and cause further cacophony on the battlefield.

Surtr shall set everything alight by striking the base of the Yggdrasil. Odin's son Vidar will seek revenge for his father's death by tearing Fenrir into two pieces. Thor's children shall salvage their father's hammer.

Two humans, Lif and Lifrasir, will wait out the end of the world and will bring forth new humanity into the world. The slain god Baldr will rise to join the new gods in a new world created from the ashes of the previous one.

And so, like Ymir's downfall gave birth to our current reality, Ragnarök will give rise to a new reality, and the cyclical nature of reality shall continue.

We shall discuss creation and Ragnarök in detail in respective chapters. Here, the purpose of summarizing these two events was to shed light on the cyclical nature of the world in Norse mythology.

### Spirits Thriving All Around Us

Animism, as we discussed earlier, is the belief that all things are essentially living things containing a spirit. Norse Paganism takes this belief and applies it to the entire world. Animism demands that everything be treated with a certain amount of respect, as everything has a role to play in the grand design.

The spirits of natural places were known as Vættir.

Norse Paganism treated everything as if it was alive, and the purpose of its rituals was to foster a harmonious relationship with these things. Yes, the gods were important as well, but so were everyday things like trees, rivers, meadows, and clouds.

**The Web Of Fate**

Finally, the last truth central to Norse mythology is fate. In Norse mythology, fate is more than just an unchangeable destiny that will come regardless of what we do or act; in Norse mythology, fate is akin to an alive being. It is active and changing, depending on the actions that you take in the immediate present. The two main forces that shape fate are known as Orlog and Hamingja.

Orlog is the base of fate. You can consider it those things that have already been determined by previous actions that are beyond your control, such as the time of your birth, the place where you live, and how your life is affected by the consequences of other people's actions.

Hamingja, also known as luck, is comprised of your conditions, your skills, your resilience, and anything else in your life that you are capable of changing through positive or negative action.

Norse Paganism is about accepting the fact that you can change your fate rather than sit idly and wait for fate to change you. Given paganism's immanent nature, it is recommended that you take positive action using your faculties to achieve the reality that you desire and in doing so, change your fate for the better.

What Kinds Of Paganism Are Being Practiced Today?

Given Norse Paganism's decentralized nature, it should come as no shock that in different regions, different types of Paganism are being followed. Some of the prominent ones include:

- Asatru
- Vanatru
- Rökkatru
- Shamanism
- Theodism
- Thursatru
- Odinism
- Lokeans
- Tribal Heathenry

Even though we're going to discuss these in great detail in a later chapter, I saw it fit to give you a basic overview of the prominent types of beliefs that are being followed today, so that you have an idea of what to expect in terms of paganism beliefs and practices.

**Asatru**

Asatru revives the ancient practices and beliefs of the old Norse faith. The word Asatru means Æsir faith, referring to the Æsir gods. The clergy in this religion are known as goðar. This religion was revitalized by Sveinbjörn Beinteinsson in 1972, to bring back the worship of the Norse deities.

Asatru's modern beliefs are along the vein of humanism and even reconstructionism, where the deities are reimagined as metaphorical rather than actual beings. However, this reconstructionist belief varies from follower to follower, as some followers still believe in the deities being actual entities. Deities venerated in Asatru include Thor, Odin, Freya, and several of the Æsir.

Asatru's beliefs emphasize one's positive actions in this world rather than transcendental actions meant to attain an afterlife. The practitioners believe in the creed "you are your deeds."

The central ritual in Asatru is known as Blót; wherein sacrifice is made to the gods and goddesses in a commemorative, communal setting through the use of alcohol. Several texts are followed by the followers of Asatru, including the words of Snorri Sturluson. Other texts that Asatruans follow include collections of runes, Eddas, books, sagas, and poems such as the Hávamál.

Those who congregate as part of Asatru are known as Kindreds. The priest of a Kindred is known as a Gothar. The congregants are known as Folk. The ceremonies performed are called Blóts, and the altars upon which the Blót is performed are known as the Stalli.

**Vanatru**

As Asatru is "true to the Æsir", Vanatru is "true to the Vanir." Vanatru takes spiritual practices inspired by the Vanir. Vanatru focuses on the Vanir-centric aspects of heathenry, including divination, being attuned to nature, folk magic, and witchcraft. Gods and goddesses venerated in Vanatru include Njord, Freya, Frey, Nerthus, Ullr, Frodi, and so forth. Since the Æsir are considered gods of order, war, civilization, and justice, and the Vanir are considered the gods of nature, those who are drawn to Vanatru tend to be more earth-centric. This is the key difference between the two practices.

In Vanatru, importance is given to the individualistic nature of worship, where each god and goddess is worshipped or venerated in a way that's unique to them.

## Rökkatru

Those who focus on the third pantheon of the gods, such as Hela, Loki, Surtr, and Jörmungandr took upon the name Rökkatru. This religion originated in New Zealand. The word Rökkatru means "worthy of the gods" or "true to the gods."

It should be noted that venerating the Rökkr gods does not mean condoning evil. The correlation of darkness with evil is a very Christian concept. When we talk about darkness in the context of Rökkatru, we are talking about necessary forces that ensure that the world is balanced. Death is not perceived as evil. Without death, there would be no cycle of life. Similarly, mischief is yet another aspect of life without which there would be no order or honor. When Surtr sets forth the gears of Ragnarök, he is not being an evil entity. He's performing his role as delegated. Without Hel to preside over her realm, there would be no one left to oversee the portion of the dead that she receives.

Other practices such as Odinism, Shamanism, Thursatru, and Theodism all fall under the umbrella of paganism, with their specific practices, beliefs, and rituals. Whatever their differences may be, the foundation remains the same: venerating the Norse gods, understanding the old creed, and becoming a better person through the religious practices that allow you to focus on the here and now.

## What Literature Can I Peruse?

Even though Norse mythology and paganism draw from a preliterate society where books were not seen as the primary source of conveying information, today, thanks to the works of devotees, we have several foundational texts available that you can peruse to give yourself a better understanding of Norse mythology and paganism.

**The Eddas and the Sagas**

Around 1200 AD, an unnamed editor compiled traditional Norse mythical poems and named his compilation The Poetic Edda. In the Poetic Edda, the poems about the gods and goddesses of old are preserved. The Poetic Edda is considered to be a very raw and unabridged compilation of Norse poetry.

However, despite their anonymous nature, the poems are arranged coherently, starting from the creation of the world. This poem is known as Voluspa.

Then, there's a poem known as the Hávamál where Odin talks to the reader directly, offering his wisdom and insights. Similarly, there are poems about the gods Frey and Thor as well.

In 1222, Snorri Sturluson took some of the stories in the Poetic Edda as well as some folklore that wasn't written in the Poetic Edda and compiled a book called Edda. Modern scholars differentiate between the two works by calling one the Poetic Edda and Snorri's work the Prose Edda.

The Prose Edda is one of the most approachable written works for someone interested in getting into Norse mythology, as they detail everything chronologically.

Similarly, the Icelandic Sagas, written in the 13th and 14 centuries, detail the stories between the settlement of Iceland until the 11th century, describing the events that took place among the Celtic and Nordic inhabitants of Iceland. These sagas offer great insight into the pre-Christian religion followed in the region as well as the culture that dominated that geographical region. These sagas provide us with accurate historical accounts of medieval Scandinavian societies and kingdoms, allowing us to make sense of what transpired historically.

## Íslendingabók

This text contains the history of Iceland and some of the earliest recorded Norse mythology about the battle of the gods. Within this book, the creation of Midgard is also detailed. This narrative text also tells us of the advancement of Christianity in Iceland during the 13th century. A database by the same name is created by a biotech company called deCODE genetics, attempting to record the genealogy of Icelandic people.

## Landnámabók

Also known as the Book of Settlements, this medieval Icelandic text describes how the Norse people settled in Iceland in the 9th and 10th centuries. Divided into five parts and told over a hundred chapters, this book contains information on important events, family histories, and settlements. It also provides genealogical accounts of the settlements and their settlers. There are stories told in the book as well which gives it a narrative structure. This book is also one of the primary sources of heathenism and the pagan religion, followed by the Norse folk.

## The Germania of Tacitus

Written in the 1st century, this is the most complete account of the religion and society of the Germanic tribes who settled in Germania. Tacitus's work provides not just the historical account of the Germanic tribes but also includes symbolism and allusive storytelling that grants us a deeper understanding of the ancient Germanic worldview. Tacitus's work is still being interpreted and reinterpreted to this day.

## Runes

These ancient alphabets that originated in Germanic and Scandinavian countries are used by many Pagans in their divination and magic rituals. According to Norse lore, Odin was directly responsible for the runes becoming available to us, as he discovered these runes as part of his trial wherein he hung from the Yggdrasil for nine days.

Understanding the history of these runes, their modern usage, and their historical context, as well as their application in divination and magical rituals, will pave the way for you to get a deeper understanding of how such symbolism relates to Norse mythology.

## Modern Research in Archaeology, History, Linguistics, and Anthropology

Lastly, stay in touch with modern discoveries of science, archaeology, history, anthropology, and linguistics as work is currently being done in the present to gain a nuanced understanding of the historical significance of Norse mythology and Norse Paganism. Every day, more discoveries pave the way for a clearer understanding of the rich history that the Norse folk have left behind.

One such way of going about it is creating a Google alert for Norse mythology news so that you can get alerted about any new developments that might take place. Another excellent method is to join a community of kindred spirits who can keep you in the loop and boost your enthusiasm in the meantime.

The more research you conduct, the more intuitively Norse Paganism will come to you. You might even feel the draw of certain gods and goddesses, allowing you the opportunity to explore your spirituality further. In doing your homework, you will uncover many mysteries that will make you question what you know about this world and completely recontextualize life as you know it.

# CHAPTER 2
# THE ORIGIN AND HISTORY OF NORSE PAGANISM

You are the living link to history. Stored deep within your soul, within the DNA that you are made of, and within your mind, there are memories of your ancestors. It might sound like I'm taking a leaf out of the *Assassin's Creed* games, but the fact remains that all of us contain a stamp, a signature, of our ancestors dating back to the first humans.

If we seek to live a more meaningful life and experience a deeper connection to our reality, it is in our interest that we learn about where we came from and who our ancestors were. To that end, we should also put on our Indiana Jones hats and go on a little archaeological expedition to unearth the origins of the old Norse way.

It is only when we learn about the origins of Norse Paganism will we realize that the chronological chain of events attests to the authenticity of the religion. We will understand that these are not just stories. Everything within these pages is not a work of fiction. The Vikings were real people. The Norse folk followed Paganism devotedly, spending their entire lives venerating the gods and goddesses they believed in. Through our understanding of their history, we will borrow some of their belief and lend credence to everything that we will learn along the way.

## What Do We Know Of Norse Paganism?

Norse Paganism as we know it today rose from the beliefs and practices of the Old Norse Pagans before Christianity pervaded Northern Europe. The acts, beliefs, and practices of the heathens of pre-Christian Scandinavia, especially during the age of the Vikings, are collectively referred to as the Norse religion. Other terms used to describe the old religion include Germanic paganism, Norse mythos, and Germanic religion.

Around the 7th century, Anglo-Saxon England was converted from Norse paganism to Christianity. Similarly, Scandinavia was converted three centuries later. After that, the Norse religion seemed to fade away in history, but despite efforts to completely wash it away, many traditions of paganism survived in Christian practices.

Most of what we know today was transcribed long after Christianity had spread through the area, which, unfortunately, means that there's no way to gauge how much Christianity influenced those transcriptions. However, there's still some pure knowledge preserved in the form of archeological records, temples of old, and burial mounds. One can also ascertain the real version of the religion and lore by cross-referencing different texts (the sagas and the Eddas) to create a coherent narrative that is relatively unsullied by the Christian influence.

The very least that we can ascertain from the reference material that we do have is an understanding of the community that thrived long ago, how it lived, how it worshiped different deities, and how their religion inculcated teachings and rites throughout their lifestyles.

Those who followed Paganism believed it to be an advocative religion of the land. The Norse people who followed it believed that their religion was supposed to evoke a kinship between them and everything around them.

The people focused on Nordic and Germanic deities, rituals, and folklore. Their animistic beliefs lend credence to the ideology that everything occupied a soul and that certain rituals would allow them to connect with that soul. As a result, they had rites, both complex and simple, that included everything from chanting to divining runes. Sometimes, the followers would sing songs up until the point that they'd reach a spiritual reverie where they would be possessed by the old gods.

Those who followed this religion were known as the Norsemen. Collectively, the Norsemen were a cluster of different groups spread throughout that geographic region. They rose to prominence during what we call the Viking Age. Several marked differences made the Norse people stand apart from the other civilizations of their time. The women, for one, were treated as equal in status. They could fight in battle, divorce their spouses, vote, and even acquire property.

There came a time when the Norse people were converted to Christianity during the Middle Ages. Before that happened, they used to ascribe to their native religion, the centerpiece of which was Norse mythology. These stories and their faith in them gave the Vikings' life a purpose and provided them with the foundation to shape their religious practices.

The creed that the Vikings followed rigorously reflected their relationship with the world. Rather than view the world as something to gain mastery over or think of it as an antagonist to their lives, they marveled at the world as it was, cherishing nature and acknowledging that earthly life was filled with struggle and hardships. Their faith celebrated it when the Norse people rose to the occasion, braved the hardships of the world, and accomplished great deeds for their and their people's benefit. If Vikings were being true to themselves and performing these great deeds, then they were upholding their creed.

When you read the word "Viking," it might conjure up an image of a bloodthirsty, barbaric warrior tearing through civilization wearing horned helmets, flailing axes, drinking mead, and destroying everything in his path. That image is nothing but Christian propaganda, meant to dismiss the rich lives of the Norse people by painting them as brutes.

In reality, the Vikings were so much more than that. They were brave warriors, seafaring raiders, conquerors, explorers, settlers, and traders originating from what is modern-day Norway, Sweden, Denmark, and Iceland. The Vikings quested through much of the world during the Viking Age (793-1066 AD). They explored North America five hundred years before Christopher Columbus did. They traveled as far as Baghdad in the East.

They conversed in the Norse language, wrote in runes, and practiced their ancestral faith.

The Vikings had a very nuanced social structure in which the hierarchy was divided between the Jarls at the top, the common folk in the middle, and the slaves at the bottom.

Those who ruled over the common folk were chieftains who had cultivated power and strength through military expertise. These chieftains commanded raiding warriors who traversed across Europe, ushering in a golden era in the Viking Age. This was before Scandinavia was a unified land. Back then, chieftains and Jarls, both small and large, ruled over certain areas. They were always competing with each other for power.

Unlike the barbarians that they're depicted as, the Vikings were a very nuanced people, strictly following a complex law.

It is because of the Old Norse poems, treatises, and sagas, available to us in written form, that were transcribed after the Viking Age that we have an idea of the faith and practices that they followed. These records grant us the understanding that the Old Norse religious beliefs, rather than being uniform throughout the region, were varied based on time and space. These varied beliefs and practices were based on social conventions and differences in environment (people who lived near the sea would have different practices compared to those who lived by the mountains). There were variations based on the profession of the people as well. Warriors, farmers, and hunters would adhere to beliefs specific to them rather than follow a general practice. Their religion was also influenced by the Viking's social contact with people who lived outside of the Nordic areas.

. . .

# The Timeline of Norse History

Let us take a brief look at the timeline of Norse history, which shall serve as the backbone of a detailed look into what the Viking Age was, and how the Norse folk thrived, spread throughout the region, and eventually disbanded because of Christianization.

## 8000 — 4000 B.C

Before this time, glaciers used to cover the region, making it impossible for people to come to Scandinavia. However, during this era, the glaciers started to retreat, allowing people to come to Scandinavia and settle down.

## 4000 B.C

Often, people traverse large distances for the sake of sustenance. Similarly, in this era, the hunting tribes pursued reindeer in Scandinavia, particularly in the southern region. These people are the ancestors of the Sami people. There are rock drawings discovered that date back to 4000 B.C.

## 1550 B.C

Tribes begin to form and settle between what is modern-day Sweden and Norway. At this time, amber was considered a commodity in those areas. A trade route known as the Amber Route formed from the Baltic Sea down to the Mediterranean. This route was named so because of the availability of amber along that route.

## 1000 B.C

Indo-European tribes come and settle down in Scandinavia. Around this time, the language that was spoken in that area, Proto-German, began forming its characteristics.

## 500 B.C

The Scandinavian Iron Age begins after contact with the Celtic civilization.

## 450—50 B.C.

Scandinavians and Celts begin trading with each other. At this time, the Celts occupied most of the European continent, competing with both Greeks and Romans for land.

## 200 B.C

The Scandinavian tribes also start their inquests, moving into Germany and Eastern Europe. By doing so, they displace the Celts in the region. The Celts, as a result, move into the British Isles and Ireland. It is here that we see the formation of Old Norse through the evolution of the north branch of the Proto-Germanic language.

## 150 B.C

As language evolved, so did inscriptions. Around this time, the first runes start to appear. What they were used for and what significance they had remains a mystery to this day. We know this much about those runes: they evolved from the Old Italic alphabets.

## 120 B.C

Many movements take place during this time: the Romans settle in Europe, and the Scandinavians, by then known as Goths, moved from Sweden into central Europe.

## 150 A.D

The evolution of boats becomes prominent. By 150 A.D., the boats began to look like how Viking boats are depicted in modern media, with masts, sails, and end-posts made of oak, planks, and ribs. They even had long oars that were looped to rowlocks. These boats evolved into fast and agile vessels, allowing swift movement on the seas.

## 325—500 A.D

Christianity starts to show up in central Europe thanks to the Romans. Germanic and Roman people engage in tribal skirmishes. Pirates start plundering and looting on the seas. The Huns weaken the Roman empire and subsequently make it fall in 476 A.D.

## 450—650 A.D

West Germanic tribes invade the British Isles and settle there.

## 550—790 A.D.

The upper eastern part of Sweden known as Uppsala becomes an economic force to be reckoned with, exporting many things like iron, fur, horses, and slaves.

## 500—1160 A.D

The Frankish tribes from the south are impeded by the Danes, who built walls to keep them out.

## 772—785 A.D.

The ruler of the Frankish Kingdom begins his campaign to exterminate pagans, including the Norse.

## 790—1066 A.D.

This is known as the Viking Age. The Vikings raid Scotland, Ireland, England, Spain, Wales, Germany, and France. The Norwegians wage battle against the Danes to gain control of Ireland. The Norse also discover Iceland in 860 A.D., then settle there. When Alfred the great forces Christianity on the Danes, the Danes and Norwegian people flee to Iceland.

By 912, Vikings take over the Northern Frankish lands. In 947, Norway starts adopting Christianity. Denmark follows Norway's lead. The Vikings settle in Greenland after Erik the Red discovers it.

In 1000, Iceland also converts to Christianity. Around that same time, Leif Eriksson discovers North America but is fended off by the natives.

Soon after, the Norse descended Normans invade Italy and Sicily and later on take over England. But after this point, the Viking invasions and inquest die down, and slowly, the belief in the old gods also dies down, bringing an end to the age of the Vikings.

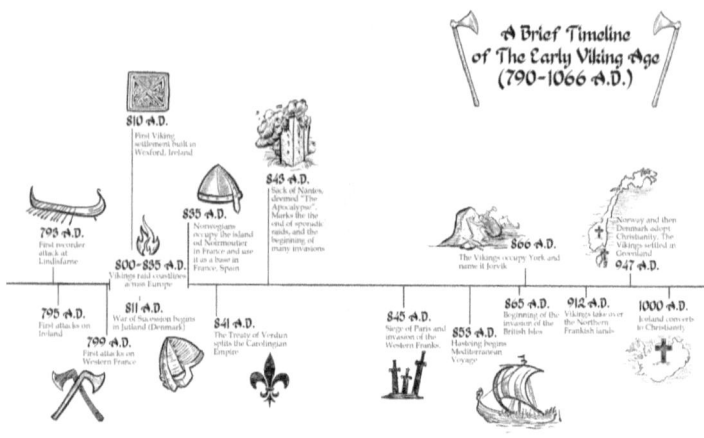

A Brief Timeline
of The Early Viking Age
(790-1066 A.D.)

810 A.D.
First Viking settlement built in Wexford, Ireland

845 A.D.
Sack of Nantes, deemed "The Apocalypse". Marks the the end of sporadic raids, and the beginning of many invasions

835 A.D.
Norwegians occupy the island od Noirmoutier in France and use it as a base in France, Spain

793 A.D.
First encounter attack at Lindisfarne

800-835 A.D.
Vikings raid coastlines across Europe

866 A.D.
The Vikings occupy York and name it Jorvik

Norway and then Denmark adorn Christianity. The Vikings settled in Greenland
947 A.D.

795 A.D.
First attacks on Ireland

811 A.D.
War of Saxonism begins in Jutland (Denmark)

841 A.D.
The Treaty of Verdun splits the Carolingian Empire

845 A.D.
Siege of Paris and invasion of the Western Franks

855 A.D.
Hastings begins Mediterranean Voyage

865 A.D.
Beginning of the invasion of the British Isles

912 A.D.
Vikings take over the Northern Frankish lands

1000 A.D.
Iceland converts to Christianity

790 A.D.
First attacks on Western France

# W hat was the Viking Age?

The Viking Age, starting from 790 A.D. and ending only with the Christianization of Scandinavia, saw the rise of Norse or Viking culture. The Norse people had an agrarian economy, relying upon farming as a source of sustenance and trade. This also made it convenient to delegate roles to different types of people. Farming was one of the primary purposes of the Norse people during the Viking age. They would farm crops like rye, oats, barley, and wheat. Their homes would be on farmsteads, enabling ease of access to their farmlands.

The work would be divided between men and women. While the men did tackle the majority of farming, the women were in charge of work inside the house. Women were charged with producing clothes and preparing food.

They would cook and bake and produce things such as cheese, milk, mead, and beer. The women would milk the animals as well. As fresh food was not always readily available, women were also charged with preserving food by salting and pickling it.

Meanwhile, the more physically demanding activities were tasked to the men. Agricultural roles such as those of fertilizing, plowing, sowing, and harvesting would fall in the domain of men.

Besides farming and agriculture, the Vikings would travel and conquer. The grandiose desire to seek fame and fortune was embedded in their nature, ushering them to travel to the far expanses of the globe to fulfill their purpose. This allowed them to discover places such as North America and Greenland.

Their style of warfare and raiding made them feared throughout the land, providing them with a competitive edge against their foes. It was this style of combat that ushered in the Viking age.

When the Vikings attacked the Lindisfarne monastery in England, which is the first recorded Viking raid, that's when the Viking Age officially began. This happened in 793. It ended in 1066 when the last Viking King known as King Harald Hardrada was defeated in the Battle of Stamford.

In the Viking age, the Vikings discovered many different people, locations, and riches as their raids, looting, colonization, and trading brought them face-to-face with their rivals in the land. But this was not all that they did. The Vikings were also founders of cities and colonies. Dublin and Normandy are two popular locations that the Vikings founded. The Vikings also colonized Iceland, which made it possible for them to colonize Greenland as well.

This might beckon you to think how such a populace of scattered tribes so few in numbers was able to conquer so much area. Well, the Vikings were characteristically brave, fierce, and courageous. They reveled in the face of danger, often taking risks that lesser warriors would not even think of. The reason they were able to conquer so much land in such a short amount of time was their ability to brave their way through any loss they suffered. Their opponents used to think that the Vikings did not fear death.

But the Viking ideology expands beyond just pilfering and pillaging; they were also peaceful traders and, as we mentioned, farmers. Sometimes, their expeditions avoided bloodshed entirely, focusing instead on bartering with the people they came across.

As glorious and fantastic as their reign was, it eventually came to an end just as all the ages preceding them did. Just as the Stone Age was consumed by the Bronze Age and the Bronze Age was overshadowed by the Iron Age, the Viking Age as well came to an end due to the shift in religion.

By the time the 11th century came around, Christianity was taking hold of most of the world, not just Scandinavia. Perhaps one of the reasons the Viking Age came to an end was that during the Viking Age, there was not a single unified ruler of the lands. Warlords and chieftains occupied specific portions of land.

The Christianization of Scandinavia didn't happen at once. It took more than a century's worth of missionary work and conquests for the Christianization to fully take effect.

But despite the efforts of the Christians to propagate their religion and eliminate Norse Paganism, it survived and is still alive today.

Why Did the Viking Age End?

There are several factors besides just Christianization that caused the Viking Age to end. The Vikings did not exactly go extinct or die out or disappear from history. They assimilated into other cultures, became residents of other countries, and assimilated into other civilizations.

**Most Vikings Didn't Leave the Nordic Lands**

The Viking Age caught traction after the fall of the Western Roman Empire, granting Vikings the opportunity to take advantage of mostly unconquered, lawless land. However, by the $11^{th}$ century, Europe was coming into its own. William the Conqueror was making the English kingdom a stronghold while the Frankish Kingdoms were morphing into the Holy Roman Empire, propagating their version of order across the lands. Back in Scandinavia, the Viking kingdoms were evolving as well, taking the shape of the medieval monarchies of Norway, Sweden, and Denmark. The rulers of these kingdoms did not see it fit to send off their warriors overseas, finally putting an end to the Viking raids in the face of the political certainty that had taken hold of Europe.

**The Vikings Assimilated into Other Societies**

The Vikings began to assimilate into the countries where they had settled. For example, in Normandy, the Frankish rules were so vexed by the constant pillage and plunder of the Vikings that King Charles of France offered them a small area of land in the early 10<sup>th</sup> century to permanently occupy. The Viking Jarl Rollo invited more of his people from Scandinavia, and here, the Norsemen assimilated with the local inhabitants.

**They Were Offered Luxury and Riches**

Christianization was not only gradual, but it also came with political advantage, material riches, influence, and diplomatic ties. Getting marked with the Christian cross allowed the converts to receive rewards and also enabled them to continue trading in Christian establishments, towns, and cities. The trade routes were controlled by Christian believers, who demanded that to continue trading, the Vikings had to give proof that they believed in Christ.

The Christian missionaries also coaxed the Vikings by saying that the Vikings had a polytheistic faith, so why not accept one more deity (the Abrahamic God and his son, Jesus Christ) when they were already worshipping multiple gods?

This gradual and constant coaxing with riches and ease eventually led to the Christianization of Scandinavia, seemingly wiping away the Norse Pagan religion.

However, as I mentioned at the start of this book, old roots run deep. It took its time, but eventually, Norse Paganism made a resurgence in the modern era, and today, thousands of followers can be found not just in Scandinavia but all over the world.

Today, in both America and Western Europe, Paganism is one of the fastest-growing religions. According to population data, Asatru is one of the fastest-growing religions in Iceland now.

Moving forward, we will take a closer and much more detailed look at the story of creation, the nine realms, and Yggdrasil. Once we understand the historical context of the events of creation and the significance that the nine realms and the World Tree hold in Norse Paganism, we will delve into the Norse calendar and study their holidays and traditions.

# CHAPTER 3
# THE CREATION OF THE COSMOS

Almost every ancient religion that has survived the ages and is still being practiced contains its unique lore that deals with questions larger than life such as "Where did we come from?" or "How did the world come to be?" or "Where will we go after we die?" Such questions are natural, and in some religions, such as Judaism, asking such questions is encouraged so that the followers can gain a closer understanding of their god, their self, and their role in the universe.

Each religion gives the story of creation a lot of significance, and it is sometimes competitively contested as to which particular creation lore aligns most with the modern scientific understanding of this universe's creation.

In Hinduism, the universe is said to have been created by the god Brahma, who fashioned everything out of himself. The stories in the Hindu Vedas tell of a lotus flower growing from Vishnu's navel with Brahma sitting atop it. Brahma then cleaves the flower into the heavens, the world, and the sky.

Greek mythology tells us another tale entirely, stating that in the beginning, there was only a singular primordial condition known as Chaos, out of which arose Earth (Gaia), the Underworld (Tartarus), Desire (Eros), Darkness (Erebus), and Night (Nyx). Together, they created the rest of the primordial creatures, such as day, the sea, and the heavens.

In Christianity, it states that in the beginning, there was nothing, and then God said, "Let there be light." And then it took him six days to create the heavens, the earth, hell, and everything else in the universe.

In Islam, similar to Christianity, Allah commanded with a singular word "Be!" all the matter that was compacted together blew apart, spreading the universe in every direction.

But what does Norse mythology tell us about the creation of the cosmos? Is there a grand fable befitting the magnificence of Norse mythology and paganism that provides a thorough explanation of the story of creation?

The answer is yes. And for all of us who ascribe to the beliefs of Norse Paganism, the good thing is that the story of creation's spiritual and metaphorical elements serves perfectly to satiate the grandest questions of all: Who are we, where do we come from, and what's our role in this universe?

An Unparalleled Story of the Birth of The Universe

In the beginning, there was just the great empty gap known as Ginnungagap. One can describe Ginnungagap as an endless abyss that existed before the creation of the nine worlds. Norse mythology has a poetic ideology that tends to demarcate the universe into a cyclical order of creation and destruction. So, as Ginnungagap existed once before the creation of anything, so too shall it exist upon the destruction of everything.

In the poem *Völuspá*, often cited as one of the most prominent poems in the Poetic Edda, the seeress describes the state of un-creation as:

> "That was the age when nothing was;
> There was no sand, nor sea, nor cool waves,
> No earth nor sky nor grass there,
> Only Ginnungagap."

The word itself is a concatenation of two words, *ginnung* and *gap*. The word ginnung abstractly means something that is charged with magic or a primordial force. The word gap pretty much means the same as it does in English. So, the barebones definition of Ginnungagap that we can form is that of a magically charged gap. Other sources translate the name to "yawning gap" or "chaotic chasm."

To the north of this great gap was the Hvergelmir that gave water to Yggdrasil, the World Tree. Not all water went to Yggdrasil. The leftover water started freezing, as the Ginnungagap was a polarized region, with its north being extremely cold and its south being hot.

As the water started freezing, the ice world of Niflheim came into existence.

And as the south of the Ginnungagap began growing hotter—one can assume, to keep up with the cooling of the north region to conserve the polarity of the gap—this heat gave birth to the land of fire, Muspelheim.

Some of the heat that emitted from Muspelheim slowly began traveling the gap, and by the time it reached Niflheim, it was nothing more than mild warmth. However, this mild warmth was enough to melt some of the ice, causing droplets of water to drip downwards into Muspelheim.

From this seemingly aberrant chaos, order began forming. As the water reached Muspelheim, sparks started emitting, causing the fire and heat to mix in the Ginnungagap. And it is here that the first sentient creations come into existence. When the iciness of Niflheim met the blazes of Muspelheim, it gave rise to Ymir. Ymir was the first of the jötunn. Ymir is also known by another name, Aurgelmir.

These mists and rime also gave birth to Auðumbla, the primeval cow. Her name means "hornless cow rich in milk" or "abundance of humming," depending upon different sources. She nourished Ymir with her milk. As for herself, she survived by licking the salt gathered on the ice of Niflheim.

Together, Ymir and Auðumbla created life in the Ginnungagap.

Two things happen in quick succession to one another.

Firstly, Ymir started sweating because of the heat coming from Muspelheim. He began sweating and as the sweat flowed under his arms, two giants—a male and a female —were born. Furthermore, Ymir, possessing the capability to produce offspring on his own asexually, joined his legs together and created a third son named Thrudgelmir. This bizarrely formed group of giants was now the first family of frost giants in the universe, also known as the jötnar. They all nourished themselves from the cow's milk.

Now, as this was happening, of course, Auðumbla, was also sustaining herself by licking off the salt from the ice. As she kept licking, some hair emerged from the melting ice. This hair was soon followed by an entire head. On the third day of her constantly licking the ice, an entire body came out.

Here was born Búri, the first of the gods. She fed Búri the same way she had fed the giants. As he had been born a fully-formed being, much like Ymir and Auðumbla, Búri did not have to go through the process of growth from childhood to adulthood. However, the cow's milk gave him quite a lot of strength.

As to how Búri managed to bear a child, it is unknown. The existence of the mother is not confirmed in the mythical texts. It could be that he created his son Borr by mating with one of the giants or from another god freed from the ice, or asexually from his own body.

Búri also had a daughter named Bestla. Her mother, most probably, was a giantess. Now, Borr married his sister, and together, they had three sons.

Here, Odin, Vili, and Vé enter the story of creation.

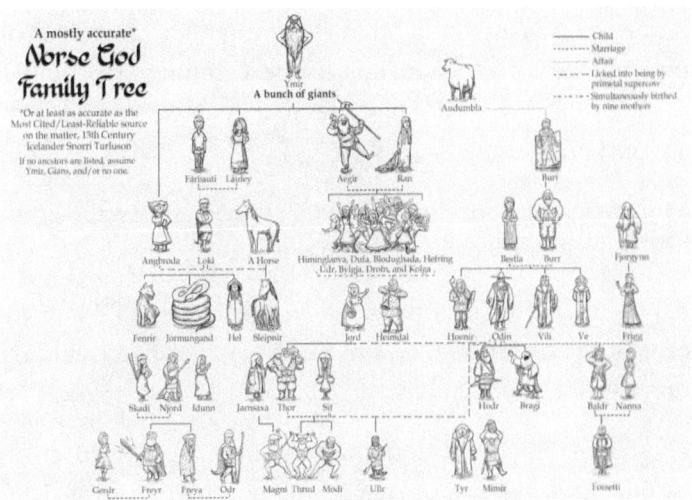

A mostly accurate* **Norse God Family Tree**

*Or at least as accurate as the Most Cited/Least-Reliable source on the matter, 13th Century Icelander Snorri Turluson

If no ancestors are listed, assume Ymir, Gians, and/or no one.

I n the Eddas, it is mentioned that Ymir was very vicious, bordering on cruelty. His behavior was depicted as that of a cruel entity. His children, in turn, were also cruel like their father. This evil behavior manifested itself when the giant and his children started oppressing the other creation, particularly the first gods. In the Gylfaginning, it is stated that when the sons of Borr finally revolted against Ymir, they slew him with such ferocity that the blood from his wounds drowned out the entire race of the frost giants except for a single giant who saved himself with his household. This giant was Bergelmir, who escaped with his wife. All the other frost giants descended from him.

This deluge of blood was not the end of Ymir. Now that the primordial giant was dead, the god-brothers decided to carry on the process of creation using Ymir's body. Such immense was his body that it required to be moved to make place for other realms in the Ginnungagap. Rather than completely shift it elsewhere, they decided to fashion a world out of it.

Ymir's flesh turned into land. His bones and teeth turned into mountains, fjords, and cliffs.

All of his blood was collected to create the water of the oceans, rivers, and lakes. His skull was used to create the dome of the sky.

They took his brain and threw it into the sky to create clouds. In some instances, it is said that both his eyes were plucked out. One became the sun, while the other turned into the moon.

All of his hair and beard were morphed into the grass and trees that covered the earth.

And yet, despite this process of intricate creation, the sky still felt barren. So, the three brothers took some sparks that were emitting from Muspelheim and trapped them in the earth's dome to appear as stars.

Knowing very well that Ymir's descendants would come for some form of revenge, the gods took the eyelashes of the giant and made a palisade around the land.

It is also mentioned that the gods sent Night and Day into the sky in horse-drawn chariots to create a full day. Night rode on a horse named Hrimfaxe. Every night he bedewed the earth. Day rode upon Skinfaxe and lit up the sky and the earth using his mane.

Some accounts stated that the Sun and the Moon were gendered and conscious beings, set along paths in the sky, forever to run fast so that they may keep outrunning the wolves who pursued them.

While Odin and his siblings were creating this new world from Ymir's corpse, worms kept coming out of the rotting body of the giant. These worms then evolved into the first dwarves. Odin, Vili, and Ve, concerned about the sky's integrity, worrying that it might fall if not held properly, told four of the dwarves to go and hold the sky up, sending them into the four major directions.

The dwarves are known as Nordi, Vestri, Sundri, and Austri, i.e., North, West, South, and East. The rest of the dwarves made their home in the land known as Svartalfheim. In time, the dwarves became experts in crafting tools. Some of the most powerful weapons in Norse mythology, such as Thor's hammer, Mjölnir, come from the dwarves.

Thus was born Midgard, also known as Middle Earth or the Middle Enclosure. Named for being placed along the middle of Yggdrasil's length, this land was to serve as a home for a new race entirely. The gods decided that they would not live here.

So they plucked some twigs from the World Tree and carved them into humanoid shapes. One was named Ask, and the other was dubbed Embla, the first man and woman.

It is fascinating to note that when the gods went about creating Midgard, they wasted no part of Ymir's corpse.

Around this time, new worlds also formed. Odin and his brothers built Asgard on the plains of Idavoll, a fabled location where the gods would meet. In yet another part, the escaped offspring of Ymir started dwelling in Jötunheimr.

Let us now take a look at the nine realms upon the World Tree, Yggdrasil, and understand the significance of each of these realms. By now, we've seen how the humans came to inhabit Midgard, how the dwarves sought refuge in Svartalfheim, how the gods went to Asgard, and how the frost giants went to Jötunnheim.

### Yggdrasil — The World Tree at the Center Of All Life

Norse Mythology considers the World Tree extremely sacred, considering it to be at the center of all creation. The origins of this tree are shrouded in mystery. The Poetic and Prose Edda mentions this tree, but there are few fables or poems that describe the creation of this tree itself. What text exists is open to different interpretations that have resulted in several different explanations.

Some claim that the Nine Realms lay along the trunk of the tree. Others deciphered that it meant that the worlds were nestled in the tree's branches. Norse artwork is very vague in terms of its representation of the worlds within the context of the World Tree, not exactly showing where the worlds existed on the tree. In general, though, all depictions, whether literary or artistic, depict it supporting the nine worlds, which is an integral belief in Norse mythology.

And where exactly did the tree itself come from? How long did it exist before the creation of the realms? Was it there in the Ginnungagap? Alas, this too is shrouded in mystery with only speculations about its origins.

The most coherent speculation that we have is that Yggdrasil was there long before any of the nine realms, any other forms of life, and even the Ginnungagap itself. All that came later. It is described, though, that the gap itself was as long as the length of the tree.

An alternate source claims that the Yggdrasil grew from a seedling and that there was a far more ancient world that existed before it.

The reason we have such obscurity about Yggdrasil is that the Norse authors considered this tree a well-known and well-understood archetype. As in its existence was broadly perceived and considered for granted or quintessential.

### Yggdrasil's Ecosystem

Besides being the cradle of the Nine Realms, Yggdrasil had a complex and diverse ecosystem, supporting different manners of fantastical life.

A humongous eagle perches atop the topmost branches of the tree. On that eagle's head, between its eyes, there was a smaller hawk. The hawk's name was Vedrfolnir. It flew between worlds to gather news and bring back vital information. Some people believe that the giant eagle was Odin himself, who possessed the ability to shift his form.

Below, in Niflheim, the world of ice, there was a dragon or serpent-like creature known as Níðhöggr who thrived on one of the roots of the Yggdrasil, gnawing at it. The implication here was that the creature was trapped by the roots. It would eventually free itself and escape at Ragnarök.

The giant eagle and the dragon bore enmity towards each other. While Níðhöggr was unable to attack the eagle, the eagle was also unable to leave its perch because of Níðhöggr's presence below.

This did not mean that the two did not communicate. There was a squirrel named Ratatosk, whom they both used to exchange slurs and insults with each other. The squirrel ran up and down the tree, passing down hate-filled messages between the eagle and Níðhöggr.

And then there were the four stags and harts who dwelled within the tree's branches. These four were known as Dainn, Dvalinn, Duneyrr, and Duraþror. They reached up to the branches and fed on their leaves. Some scholars connote their existence to that of the four seasons, the major elements, or the directional winds.

Lastly, upon the destruction of the world as a result of Ragnarök, two humans named Lif and Lifþrasirwill seek refuge in the tree, surviving the destructive events of the end of the realms. There they shall survive on the tree's leaves. Then they will emerge, much like Ask and Embla once did, and continue the cycle of creating new humans in a post-Ragnarök new world.

**The Sacredness of Yggdrasil**

Ancient Germanic religions such as Norse Paganism held sacred trees in the highest regard. Trees had symbolic, spiritual, and metaphorical strength in these old European religions.

Yggdrasil was considered the ultimate sacred tree, the embodiment of the highest order of holiness. This was its primary function. The support it provided the nine realms was a result of its holiness.

Sacred trees such as Yggdrasil were believed to connect the realms of mortal men with those of the gods and the realm of the dead. People prayed at designated sacred trees to ask favors from higher powers and to remember those who had passed.

Sacred trees were believed to be sites where sacrifices to the gods were conducted. Even Odin, the All-Father, sacrificed himself by hanging from Yggdrasil in his search for wisdom. The ultimate sacrifice by the ultimate god to the ultimate symbol of sacredness. In his words, according to the poem Hávamál:

> "I know that I hung on a windy tree
> Nine long nights,
> Wounded with a spear, dedicated to Odin,
> Myself to myself,
> On that tree of which no man knows
> From where its roots run."

## The Root Wells of Yggdrasil

Yggdrasil required a source of water to feed itself. The three main sources of water that Yggdrasil drew from were known as the well of Mimir, Hvergelmir, and the well of Urd.

Mimir's well has a fascinating backstory behind it. Mimir's head sits next to the well. The well itself is infused with Mimir's powers. Anyone who drinks from the well will get Mimir's powers and would be able to decipher ancient knowledge.

Mimir's backstory goes back to creation itself. Considered to be the wisest of gods, Mimir's knowledge expands to limits far beyond even Odin himself, who is a powerhouse of knowledge as well. He is the son of a giant named Bölþorn. His sister, Bestla, married Borr.

When war broke out between the Æsir and the Vanir, Mimir was beheaded by the Vanir and his body was left to decay. His head was sent to Odin, presumably as a message. Odin, knowing very well the station Mimir held in the realm of knowledge, tried to preserve the head and even went as far as to succeed, bringing Mimir's head back to life.

After being rescued, Mimir was given charge of a well that came to be known as Mimir's well or Mimisbrunnr.

Odin tried to reason with Mimir's head, begging him for wisdom. The two had mutual respect and held each other in high regard. One could even venture to say that they were friends. They held long talks with each other, pondering over the wisdom of the universe.

Odin pleaded with Mimir to allow him to drink from the well, but Mimir demanded that there should be a sacrifice to gain the privilege of drinking from the well. And so it was that Odin sacrificed his eye and threw it into the bottom of the well to attain wisdom.

The very same well that nourishes one of the roots of Yggdrasil.

The second well, bubbling in Niflheim, was Hvergelmir. This well was considered to be the source of major rivers. It is within this well that Níðhöggr the dragon dwelled, constantly gnawing away at the root of the tree to free himself. His venom started seeping into the root of the world tree gradually.

The third well, the well of fate, was a place where the Norns met. These were the goddesses put in charge of tending to the tree. They could also tell the future and manipulate a person's fate. It is said that the Norns deciphered the fate of all beings and would etch it on Yggdrasil itself.

Yggdrasil underwent decay as time went on, what with the dragon chewing its roots and seeping its venom into the tree, the squirrel Ratatosk also using its rodent teeth to weaken the tree, and the four stags constantly eating away the leaves.

The Norns in the well of Urd tended to the tree and made sure to restore it by pouring water over its rotting wood. But try as they might, eventually, the tree will succumb to decay, catalyzing Ragnarök itself. Of course, after that battle, it will flourish and return to its previous healthy status.

**The Nine Realms**

The colossal World Tree nestles the Nine Worlds, home to different beings and species, such as the gods, the elves, and the dwarves. These realms include:

- Midgard, where humans dwell in their civilization.
- Asgard, home of the Æsir gods.
- Vanaheim, the realm where the Vanir gods lived.
- Jötunheimr, a world filled with frost giants.
- Niflheim, the primeval world of ice.
- Muspelheim, the primordial world of fire.
- Alfheim, the realm of the elves.
- Nidavellir/Svartalfheim, the sanctuary realm of the dwarves.

- Helheim, the world of the goddess Hel, where the dead dwell.

## Midgard

Once it was populated by Ask and Embla, the newly formed Midgard soon became home to the rest of the humans who descended from Ask and Embla. The Bifrost connects Midgard to Asgard, allowing the gods to access this realm.

There is much symbolism at play here. Midgard does not only represent Earth but the middle ground between order and chaos. Within Midgard, it is peaceful, hospitable, safe, and inhabitable, allowing humans to thrive in order. Outside the palisade built from Ymir's eyebrows, there is chaos in the form of dangerous creatures, giants, and a harsh climate.

There is yet another layer to this metaphor of order and chaos. Two figures from Norse mythology play an important role in Midgard's fate. One is the god of thunder, Thor, seen as the protector of Midgard and a champion of its people. The other is Jörmungandr, the world serpent coiled around Midgard. Thor represents order, whereas the serpent represents chaos.

While Thor was seen as a favorable figure to Midgard, often traveling there with many companions and protecting this realm from dangers, Jörmungandr was the danger itself, prophesied to destroy Midgard during Ragnarök. Jörmungandr was born to Loki and the giant Angrboða. He had a brother Fenrir and a sister Hel, both of them immensely powerful beings. These three siblings would inevitably bring the destruction of the world. In an attempt to delay Ragnarök, Odin separated these three beings. He threw Jörmungandr into the seas of Midgard.

Instead of perishing, the serpent grew in size and became so huge that he encircled the world completely, creating a circumference around it and then biting upon his tail. Upon Ragnarök, Thor, representing order, would face Jörmungandr representing chaos, and together they'd fight to the death. Thor would crush the serpent's skull and kill it but also die due to the serpent's venom.

## Asgard

This spectacular home to the Æsir gods was one of the most written-about worlds in the Eddas. This is where Odin dwelled with the rest of his kin. Those who died honorable deaths also came to this land to dine in Valhalla.

Asgard was majestic. It had beautiful halls, serene fields of green, and lustrous forests. It was protected with fortifications. Everything about it spoke of grandeur. Its halls had hundreds of rooms. Its lunches were lavish. The essence of magic was imbued in this world, shaping it into a sort of utopia.

As far as its creation is concerned, the historical accounts give a lot of detail about how Midgard was formed, but there's not a lot of information given about the rest of the realms.

The god Heimdall watched over from the Bifrost to ensure that no one would assault Asgard. However, this was not the only form of protection Asgard had. Back when the Æsir and the Vanir fought each other, Asgard's walls were destroyed.

So, the gods hired someone to build the walls better than they were. This mason arrived with a single horse and claimed that he could build the wall within a year. He stated that as a reward for his timely job, he would marry Freya. If he lost, he said, he would do the entire work for free.

Freya did not want to marry this strange mason. Loki took the matter into his hands to reassure Freya. He said that it would be impossible to build a wall in a year without anyone's help.

But the strange thing was, this man and his horse worked very fast, and they were well on their way to finishing before the deadline. This put Loki in a tight spot, as he had been the one to prompt the gods into accepting the bet.

Now, on the last day, when merely a couple of slabs were left to be placed, Loki shifted into a mare and seduced the man's horse. It was because of his horse that the man was able to work so quickly and drag the massive slabs so efficiently. It isn't explicitly mentioned what Loki did with the seduced horse. At least, not so much in words. It does say in Gylfaginning that the horses ran together for the rest of the night until dawn, but here's the kicker. Loki disappeared after that.

But now that this stranger's plan had been thwarted and he was unable to finish the wall, he revealed his true identity as that of a giant named Gangleri. He had disguised himself as a mason to trick the gods into marrying him to Freya.

The gods killed him. The wall had been built, and Freya was safe.

As for Loki, well, he reappeared after many months with an eight-legged foal. Its name was Sleipnir. Loki gifted this horse to Odin.

There are several realms within Asgard itself. Some of them include:

- Valhalla, the hall with more than five hundred rooms where the Einherjar, the brave warriors who died in battle, came to dine with Odin after their death. This hall was a place of endless merriment and drinking and feasting and fighting.
- Hlidskjalf, which was a throne in Odin's palace from where he could look into all the realms.
- Bilskirnir, the grandest hall in all of Asgard, where Thor lived, celebrated, and feasted.
- Thrúdheim, the place within Asgard where Thor ruled.
- Fólkvangr, a field belonging to Freya where she welcomed those who died in battle. According to lore, Freya gets to pick the brave warriors who died in battle first. Half of them went to Fólkvangr while the other half went to Valhalla.
- Breidablik, where Baldur lived. It was a bright place where evil could not exist.
- Himinbjorg, a place on the border of Asgard near the Bifrost where Heimdall lived.

Unlike Greek mythology, where the gods had to share a single mountain, Asgard was huge and had realms within itself where each god could thrive and rule.

**Vanaheim**

This realm is home to the Vanir gods. The Vanir are a race of gods as old as the Æsir. They are the masters of fertility, wisdom, magic, and sorcery. They are also known to be tellers of the future. Vanaheim, unlike the other realms, is shrouded in mystery. No one exactly knows what it looks like or where in the hierarchy of the realms it is placed.

One of the prominent events in the history of the Vanir is the war they had with the Æsir gods. The Vanir destroyed the fortifications of Asgard and breached into the land. One of the reasons this war erupted was because both races of gods had opposing views on rules and societal structure. The Æsir believed that the world should follow strictly the rules laid down by the lawmakers, while the Vanir believed that the world should have a much more laidback attitude.

An example of this is the marriage between siblings. Æsir gods completely prohibited thi,s whereas the Vanir commonly married among siblings. Njord, a Vanir god, was married to his sister. Together they were parents to Frey and Freya, who also married each other.

Upon the end of the war, Njord, Frey, and Freya were sent to Asgard as a token of peace. The marriage between Frey and Freya was annulled, and they were married to other gods. Hoenir and Mimir were also sent to the Æsir by the Vanir.

### Jötunheimr

Home to the giants, this realm comprises wilderness, dense forests, rocky plains, and snowy regions. The giants survive on a diet of fish that they get from the outer shores of the ocean. Jötunheimr is depicted as a barren place where fertile land is nonexistent.

Some of the most prominent characters of Norse mythology come from this land. Loki is one of the Jötunn.

As far as the land itself is concerned, it is a place where chaos rules. The place is home to deception. Nothing is as it seems there. Normal laws of the universe do not apply in Jötunheimr. Realities and dreams tend to intermix there, leaving a visitor perplexed.

## Niflheim

This dark, cold region in all the realms is one of the two primeval worlds that existed before creation. Here, the bubbling spring Hvergelmir served as a river, providing water to the root of Yggdrasil. This land is inhabited by ice giants. It is said that most cold rivers that flow in the world come from Niflheim.

## Muspelheim

This land of fire is one of the primeval worlds that caused the creation of the universe. This fiery place, burning with lava, flames, sparks, and spread with ash, is where the fire demons, fire giants, and the giant Surtr lived.

Surtr bore enmity to the Æsir. Upon Ragnarök's arrival, he will ride out with his sword and attack Asgard, turning it into a hellscape. His destruction will be the final flourish to the chaos and desolation that Ragnarök will cause.

## Alfheim

Cradled right next to Asgard, this realm is home to the most beautiful creatures in Norse mythology, the light elves. Frey rules over the light elves, who in turn serve as the guardian angels of common folk. You may even consider them minor gods in the sense that they have control over magic and fertility. They can use this prowess to help human beings. Like the muses in Greek mythology, the elves of Alfheim can help poets and writers with inspiration. They also have a keen understanding of music and can assist musicians in coming up with symphonies, melodies, and songs.

Given the bright nature of the elves and their role as assisters, some scholars have concluded that the light elves are the Norse equivalent of angels.

## Nidavellir

The realm of the dwarves is cavernous, filled with mines, forges, and resources that the dwarves can use for their crafting. The dwarves have historically provided many of the strongest weapons and artifacts that the gods have used. Odin's magic ring and his Gungnir spear came from the dwarves as well as Thor's hammer, Frey's ship, and the enchanted chain that bound Fenrir, the wolf.

## Helheim

Ruled over by Hel, the goddess of the realm of death, and daughter of Loki, this land is cold, dark, depressing, desolate, misty, and downright unpleasant. There is no escaping from this realm as the impassable river Gjoll hinders any who try to break free. Once someone enters Helheim, they cannot leave, not even if they are gods. Odin couldn't save his son Balder from Helheim.

Those who die of disease or old age and those whose deaths were not as a result of battle go to Helheim. Garm, a humongous beast, and Modgud, a female guardian, guard the entrance to this realm. At the edge of this world sits the giant Hræsvelgr, making the wind blow in his eagle form.

At the end of the world, Hel will sail to Asgard alongside Loki in a ship made from the fingernails and toenails of the dead. Her realm and the residents of her realm will play a significant role in Ragnarök.

We have discussed at length the creation of the cosmos, the details about the nine realms, and the mysticism of Yggdrasil. Moving forward, we are going to understand the Norse gods and the Norse calendar and holidays, allowing ourselves to immerse further in the rich lore of Norse mythology. It is only through understanding the lore and its implications that we can integrate Norse Paganism into our lives.

# CHAPTER 4
# THE NORSE CALENDAR AND PAGAN HOLIDAYS

Cast your mind back to the old Norse days with me and imagine a world where science and technology have not made any of the modern strides yet. There are no tall buildings, no such concept as electricity, and when night falls, it is not bright neon lamps or arc-sodium lights that illuminate the villages but the clear night sky with its myriad stars and the luminescence of the moon.

To anyone who lived during that time, the world was filled with mysticism, with faith being the propelling force behind most beliefs instead of factual scientific data. Magic was seen as a likelier explanation of the wonders of the cosmos as observed from the standpoint of an observer looking up into the sky.

It is a feeling that we cannot perceive, knowing what we know. To someone living in the Norse era, the sun set in the west and rose in the east. To them, this was certain. Irrefutable. Of course, the sun came up from behind the mountains, and of course, it dipped into the sea. They did not know the orbiting nature of the earth around the sun.

Their worldview was that of unbridled fantasy and belief in forces and beings far more powerful than themselves. A purer, stronger belief that left no place for doubt, allowing the average folk to delve freely into the depths of their religious beliefs.

As time went on and as the theories and knowledge of the European world pervaded, these beliefs gradually dwindled, aligning with the modern worldview that we know today, a world where astronomy is a science and explains the details of how constellations are formed, what planets are, and why forces like gravity exist.

But let's go back to that old age, where common folk believed in uncommon things—there was still a semblance of order to their actions. They followed a calendar devised from the phases of the moon, dividing the year into twelve months of thirty days, and in leap years, there were four extra days every fourth summer called the Sumarauki. They adhered to solstices and equinoxes as most civilizations did at that time.

The Norse people lived so far up north that they noticed the solstices and equinoxes far more clearly, as these astronomical events are much more visible in the northern regions of the earth. This allowed them to predict the arrival of different seasons, which were critical for their farming and agriculture. Another stark difference between them and us is that they only had two seasons: summer and winter.

**The Lunar Calendar**

Norse folk made sense of the passage of time through their lunar calendar, wherein they counted each month from new moon to new moon or full moon to full moon. Even though the moon had a very critical role in their understanding of time, the sun played a more important role. To understand why this was so, you must know that Scandinavia is and was a very cold and dark place. The sun was heralded as a bringer of light and warmth, allowing the people to grow their crops.

Dividing the year into summer and winter, the Norse people had designated moon cycles as the following months:

**Skammdegi — the Winter Months**

- **Gormánuður** — known as slaughter month, lasting from mid-October to mid-November. In the olden days, slaughtering an animal was a complex task as there was no way to refrigerate its meat. You had to either cook the entire animal or risk spoiling it. But when the weather was cool, the meat was able to stay fresher for a longer time. The winter months were times when it was very hard to feed farm animals, given that they were utilizing valuable crops. So, to deal with this, the farmers slaughtered most animals other than their breeding stock. The cold of October and November allowed them to preserve this meat for longer. It is in this month that a feast called Winter blót is held to honor Frey to thank him for the harvest.
- **Ýlir** — lasting from mid-November to mid-December, the Yule month, is connected to Odin.

Yule comes from one of Odin's names, Jolnir, which originates from the word Jol. During this time, Odin traveled a lot around Midgard, visiting the locals. Kids filled their socks with hay to feed Sleipnir, Odin's horse, so that Odin would give them a gift. This month also has significance in terms of fertility and cultivation of the earth.

- **Mörsugur** — literally known as "fat-sucker month," was between mid-December to mid-January. In the harsh winter months, the Norse folk had to survive the months by consuming animal fat. This was a time when nothing grew on the land in terms of crops. Besides animal fat, people consumed bone marrow as well. Winter solstice was held this month.

- **Þorri** — from mid-January to mid-February, the frozen snow month was observed, its name coming from Thor. During this month, the feast known as Þorrablót was held. The night before this month begins, the women walk outside their homes and welcome the month inside as a guest. Some speculate that Þorri was a winter spirit or an entity. This month was also observed as a month for men, and men could choose a day within this month to be celebrated. At this time of the year, people used to eat some hardy food such as sheep heads, rotten sharks, testicles of rams, and jelly made from meat. Liquor was also consumed heavily in this cold month.

- **Góa** — between mid-February and mid-March, this month was celebrated. This month was observed as women's month. It was the penultimate month of winter.

- **Einmánuður** — from mid-March to mid-April, the lone month was observed. It was referred to as the single month or the lone month because it was the final month before summer arrived. This month was dedicated to young boys.

## Náttleysi — the Summer Months

- **Harpa** — starting from mid-April and ending in mid-May, this was considered the first month of the Norse calendar year. This month was dedicated to girls, as Harpa is a girl's name. As for which deity this month was named after, it is unclear as there are no records of a goddess existing under that name. The summer blót was held in this month, serving as a feast in veneration of Odin to ensure that victory comes to warriors and all the travelers reach their destinations safely.
- **Skerpla** — from mid-May to mid-June, this month, named after a forgotten goddess, was the second month of summer and considered a time of new life.
- **Sólmánuður** — the third summer month from mid-June to mid-July was when summer solstice was held. This was the brightest time of the year in Scandinavia, with some days even lasting for twenty-four hours. That's why this month got the name "the sun month."
- **Heyannir** — the fourth summer month from mid-July to mid-August was a time for haymaking. This was when the people dried and harvested the hay. In some parts of Scandinavia, this month was known as worm's month or snake's month. One

can assume this was so because these creatures infested the harvested hay.

- **Tvímánuður** — from mid-August to mid-September, the Tvímánuður, meaning two months arrived, heralding sunny times, fall foliage, and a cold snap in the air. People harvested grains during this month. This was the final month of summer.

- **Haustmánuður** — from mid-September to mid-October, people observed the month of Haustmánuður, which was treated more as an autumn month and a preparatory month for winter. People believed that summer was behind and that now it was time to harvest and brace for the upcoming winter months.

All the months of the Norse calendar began with the same day of the week. This calendar gave the Norse folk a timeline to observe Norse holidays and celebrations.

**The Norse Holidays**

Festivals and holidays are plentiful in the Norse calendar. The Icelandic people loved to celebrate. Their primal lifestyle came with its fair share of difficulties, both in battle and in times of peace, but whenever they overcame their adversities, they made sure to mark that occasion with a well-deserved celebration.

- **Þorrablot** — This mid-winter celebration, also known as husband's day, was a time when people honored the fathers and husbands. Held in honor of the winter spirit Þorri and the god Thor, this festive celebration included locals coming together to sing, dance, and eat specific delicacies that they washed down with strong alcohol. Locals used to eat Þorrablot particular foods such as rotten shark meat, boiled sheep's head, picked ram's testicles, wind-dried white fish, and dung-smoked lamb. Then they drank a potent drink known as Black Death. After dinner, the folks sang together heartily, played games with each other, and partied until the morning.

- **Góublót** — This holiday took place on the first day of Góa in honor of all women, especially mothers and wives. This celebration also served to mark the coming end of winter.
- **Sigrblót** — Taking place on the first day of Harpa, this holiday was to mark the victory of light over dark. In other words, the victory of summer over winter. During this holiday, people made offerings to Freya.
- **Mid-summer**— The celebration of the light, warmth, and one's connection to the earth, was a festival for the summer solstice. People joyously venerated fertility, magic, and light during this celebration. The nature of the celebrations included feasting, dancing, and building a bonfire.
- **Alfarblót**— This holiday marked the first day of winter. There were certain reasons for this much more sober celebration. The people had done their last harvest of the year and so were thanking Freya for bestowing fertility upon the land. It was a much more toned-down celebration, mostly held inside the privacy of people's homes. Rather than the men, the women of the house led the celebrations.

- **Yule** — The Norse folk celebrated the midwinter solstice by drinking, feasting, and sacrificing to the gods for twelve consecutive days. This holiday was in celebration of Odin, believing that he would ride across the night and visit them in their homes.
- **Dísablót** — This holiday honored female deities including the goddesses, the ancestors, the Valkyries, and the prominent figures of Norse mythology. As to when this was celebrated, it's a bit unclear. Some sources stated that it was celebrated at the start of the winter while other sources claimed that it was celebrated at the end. And then some say that it was celebrated on both.

**Heathen Holidays**

Building upon the existing lore of the festivals, the calendar, and the significance of certain days, a Heathen calendar was created by Steven McAllen in the late twentieth century. However, this calendar took inspiration from the Wiccan wheel of the year and then assigned Nordic names to celebrations that had already existed within Northern Europe.

It is considered by some to be a more contemporary alternative option for celebrating holidays. Some contemporary heathenry borrows from both Wicca and paganism and has evolved into an amalgamation of different religions. This particular calendar designates the following days for the following celebrations:

- **Disting/ Dísablót** — On the 2nd of February, the Dísablót celebrations marked new beginnings and preparing the crops for planting.
- **Ostara** — On the 21st of March, Ostara was celebrated to mark the rejuvenation of the land and to celebrate fertility.
- **May Eve** — On the 30th of April, May Eve was celebrated, associated with Frey and Freya, to celebrate fertility and the arrival of spring.
- **Midsummer** — on the 21st of June, Midsummer was celebrated by burning corn dollies, playing music, and dancing around bonfires to mark the summer solstice.
- **Frey Feast** — On the 1st of August, people thanked Frey for the yearly harvest and baked a loaf of bread as an offering to Frey.
- **Fall Feast** — On the 23rd of September, upon the Autumn equinox, the coming of Fall as well as the second harvest of the season, was celebrated. This celebration marked a time for gathering food for the upcoming winter months.
- **Winter's Nights** — On the 31st of October, this celebration took place to mark the end of the harvest season and to herald the time for hunting animals. This celebration venerated Hel, the goddess, as this was considered a time when the veil between the world of the living and the world of the dead thinned down.
- **Yule** — Celebrated between the 20th of December and the 1st of January, Yule marked the beginning and end of all things. This was considered the time when the gods were closest to Midgard and when the dead returned to the earth to feast with

their living family members. It was a time when magic was thought to course freely through the earth.

**The Days of the Week**

The fascinating story of the Norse calendar doesn't just end here. Did you know that the days of the weeks were named after the Norse gods?

- **Monday** was known as Mandag, named after the god Mani. Mani's parents named him after the moon, which made him suffer a terrible fate in turn. He had to drag the moon across the sky with his chariot for his entire life.
- **Tuesday** was known as Tirsday, a day devoted to Odin's son, Tyr, whom many knew as a god of war and a god of the sword. The Norse folk, especially the Vikings, held the belief that the best day to start a war was Tyr's day.
- **Wednesday** was named after Odin himself. It was called Onsdag. To commemorate this day, it is recommended to indulge oneself in the pursuit of knowledge, as Odin did. Odin's old name was Woden, which is where the name Wednesday comes from.
- **Thursday** was Torsdag, known as Thor's day. Hammer in hand, riding his chariot, emitting the roar of thunder, Thor was a symbol of divinity, power, strength, and bravery. It was believed that Thursday was the best day to do magic, as magic was fortified on this day.

- **Friday** or Fredag was dedicated to Frigg and Freya, the beautiful goddesses of love, fertility, and innate connection with one's inner self.
- **Saturday**, although gets its name from Saturn, was known as Lordag or Laugardagen, a day devoted to washing one's clothes. The Norse folk were very careful about their clothes, ensuring that they were clean.
- **Sunday,** aka Sondag, was named after Sol, the sun goddess. The gods did not like the pride with which Sol had been named after the sun, so they punished her for eternity by making her pull the sun in her chariot.

Although these customs, celebrations, festivals, and the old calendar diminished in use just as the Norse folk, many elements of them are still retained within our Gregorian calendar. We still use the same name for days, for instance. The Nordic celebrations affected many of the Christian holidays. Yule, for instance, heavily influenced Christmas. Originally, December wasn't even considered a time when Jesus was born. But to proliferate the teachings of the church, Christian missionaries tried to infuse Christian teachings with pagan beliefs to make them more palatable for those considering converting to Christianity.

Regardless, the revival of Norse Paganism in recent years has seen to it that these old rituals, customs, celebrations, festivals, and holidays are also revived and observed. Devotees and adherents to Paganism-centric beliefs, such as Asatru, follow the holidays and celebrations as described in the Norse calendar.

With the calendar and its celebrations clear to us, we will now move on to take a detailed look at the gods and goddesses of the Norse pantheon, understand their lineage, powers, and symbols associated with them, and how we can venerate them. Everything that we have learned so far brings us closer to a concise and thorough understanding of Norse mythology, the beliefs of paganism, the ideologies promulgated by this belief system in modern Paganism, and how all of these can be integrated into your life.

Learning about the gods will bring us one step closer to becoming better Pagans. Knowing particularly which god or goddess possesses what traits and abilities will allow us specificity in terms of whom to venerate and how to venerate them to ask for their help.

# CHAPTER 5
# THE NORSE PANTHEON OF GODS AND GODDESSES

I f there is one thing that can be said with certainty about the Norse gods, it is that they were magnificent in their splendor. And it was not just a predetermined grandeur such as the one we see in Greek mythology, where luxury was almost considered a requirement for the gods and goddesses of the Greek pantheon. Rather, the Norse gods and goddesses were rugged in their powers, more primal, and more connected to the realms they oversaw and the roles they were delegated. The physical characteristics of the gods were earned through toil and extraneous effort rather than just handed to them at godhood.

Odin, for instance, had to lose an eye to transcend his reserves of knowledge. When he hung from Yggdrasil, a spear was pierced through his side, scarring him. His visage and appearance were that of an aged man, giving his wisdom an extrinsic manifestation.

Thor, similarly, had an immense muscular and broad build courtesy of his adventures, his role as the god of thunder, and his reputation as a fierce warrior.

Goddesses such as Hel and Frey evoked respective emotions in the hearts of their believers. Hel drew fear because of her appearance, whereas Frey, one of the most beautiful goddesses, made onlookers' jaws drop in sheer awe.

They were fully-realized, deep personalities with redeeming traits, profound powers, and even some flaws such as becoming too prideful, resorting to wrath, or being conniving. But these flaws did not take away from their magnificence. Rather, they accentuated it by showing us that the gods, in whose image we were made, were also capable of folly at times, making us appreciate them more, resonate with them, and revere them for their fortitude, wit, wisdom, strength, and beauty.

The two primary factions of gods are the Æsir and Vanir. Historical sources such as the Eddas have paid more heed to the Æsir. What we know of the Vanir is all mentioned in sources within the context of the Æsir gods.

The Æsir and the Vanir were rivaling parties, which even led to a war between them, a war that ended with both sides exchanging "hostages" as a token of peace.

Both factions live in their respective realms. The Æsir have made their home in Asgard, while the Vanir live in Vanaheim.

Odin is the strongest and the most revered of the Norse gods. Ruler of the Æsir, he is married to Frigg, the queen of Asgard.

Every god, whether they were a Vanir or an Æsir, had unique characteristics that made them stand out from the rest. Loki was a mischief-monger, forever bent on creating trouble in the most creative of ways. Thor, who thought more with brawn than brain, was quick to anger. Freya, aware of her unmatched beauty, was always looking for new jewelry.

You might be wondering how the gods in the Norse pantheon could be as strong as they were and how they were immortal. The goddess of spring and rejuvenation, Iðunn, provided the gods with apples that ensured their long life.

Unlike the gods of other religions, the Norse gods did not cut themselves off from the rest of the world, forever residing in their heaven like home. Instead, they routinely made trips to other realms, interfering in affairs with the humans, and also interacting with other races such as the elves, dwarves, and giants.

As you'll know more about the gods, you are bound to pick a favorite, whether consciously or subconsciously. Let that happen. Let the magic take you.

Without further ado, let's talk of the gods.

# Baldur — The God of Light

**B**aldur — The God of Light

Said to be the most beloved of all gods, goddesses, and humans, Baldur represented light. And not just represented; because of his beauty, his grace, and his cheerful nature, he actually emanated light. It was said that such was his beauty that even the prettiest of flowers bowed as he walked past them. In Norse mythology, he was perceived as the epitome of perfection, not only in appearance but also in his benign wisdom.

He was very meek and mild, always speaking in a calm and tender voice. Where he lived was a place known as

Breidablik, the cleanest and brightest place in Asgard. His hall was considered the most resplendent in all of the realms.

His powers included the gift of wisdom and deep knowledge. He had precognition and could also make prophecies. His bright nature and his wisdom made him the arbiter of conflicts among men and gods.

It is no surprise that Baldur gets wisdom and knowledge, and light as part of his traits. He was, after all, the son of Odin and Frigg. Baldur had a loving wife named Nanna, and they had a child named Foresti, who was the god of peace and justice.

But that is where the cheery disposition of his story ends.

Once, Baldur's dreams began turning to nightmares showing his death. When he went to his mother, one of the wisest gods in the realm, and confided in her about this strange occurrence, Frigg became extremely worried about her son. A mother's love is a powerful force. Perhaps there is no force more powerful than it. Such was her adoration for her son that Frigg, to ensure Baldur's safety, went one by one to every single thing in the universe, taking an oath from them promising that they would not harm Baldur.

And all things agreed to this polite request put forth by Frigg.

Now, Baldur was invincible. His invincibility became a source of fun to the rest of the gods. So confident were they that nothing would harm him they would throw weapons at him and fling random things at him just to watch them bounce off him, leaving him completely unscathed.

For a little while, Baldur himself was content with this drastic measure, no longer concerned about dying as he had seen in his dreams.

But Loki, the trickster god, decided that this was the right time to create chaos through his mischief. Innocently he approached Frigg, asking her if she had indeed made everything take an oath in the universe or not. He feigned concern to appeal to her better nature and to come off as harmless. When her guard was down, she casually mentioned that the only thing she didn't take an oath from was the harmless and tiny mistletoe. She said that she considered it far too harmless to even take an oath from it. How could mistletoe harm Baldur?

But this sliver of information was almost too much for Loki, who fashioned a lethal spear out of mistletoe. He went to the blind god Hodr, who was also Baldur's brother, coaxing him into joining the let's-throw-things-at-Baldur-because-he-won't-be-hurt party. He gave Hodr the spear and sent him forth and watched with twisted glee as Hodr flung the spear.

Instead of bouncing off of Baldur, the spear pierced him and killed him on the spot.

All of Asgard fell in silent shock. The gods were torn with agony, having lost their favorite god. But they did not want to simply give up. After all, Baldur might be dead, but he was in Hel, the realm of the dead. Surely, he could be brought back from there through divine intervention.

Odin's son Hermod, Baldur's brother, decides to make the perilous trip down to Hel to appeal to Hel, the goddess of the realm of death, to return Baldur. He made the trip on

Odin's horse Sleipnir and rode down Yggdrasil till he reached the dark world of Hel.

Here he found his brother, miserable, stolen of his light, grim, pale, weakened, sitting in the seat of honor next to Hel's throne. Hermod, being a diplomatic being, asked Hel if she could release Baldur. Hel, of course, denied this at first, but after much persuasion on Hermod's behalf, she finally agreed on one twisted condition: Every living being in the universe would have to mourn and weep for Baldur to prove that he was as universally beloved as the gods claimed. Only then would she free him.

So Hermod went from Hel with a huge task on his shoulders, asking every being in the universe to weep and mourn for Baldur. But the whole world did indeed mourn him truly, and upon his asking, everything in the world did mourn for Baldur except one. When Hermod went to the goddess Þökk, she refused to weep for Baldur. It's believed that Þökk was Loki in disguise. And so it was that with Loki/ Þökk's refusal to weep that Baldur was forever doomed to remain in Hel's dark realm.

It's kind of ironic that the god of light would have to perish in the realm of darkness. It is also sickeningly depressing that the most beloved and friendliest of all gods would have to die in front of his family.

The gods decided to give Baldur a befitting funeral. They placed his body on the mightiest ship in Asgard and set it out to the sea. The ship was set ablaze as it went out into the sea.

Grief-stricken, Baldur's wife, Nanna, threw herself into the burning ship, not wanting to live a life without her husband. She hoped as she burned that she would be resurrected with Baldur after the events of Ragnarök. The gods assembled at the funeral threw all of Baldur's things in the fire, even his horse. As the ship burned and was carried off by the sea, the earth shook.

But do not despair too much about the death of the god of light. It is prophesied that he will return from Hel after Ragnarök and will be taking his place as the ruler of the new world alongside his blind brother Hodr.

This is not where the story ends, however. There is still the matter of Loki, who orchestrated Baldur's death. During a heated argument with the gods in the Aegir's halls, Loki confessed to being responsible for Baldur's death, which enraged the gods to such an extent that they chained Loki to massive rocks and placed a dangerous snake over his face. The venom dripped from the snake's fangs atop Loki, causing him unbearable pain. It is said in lore that Loki's punishment would last until Ragnarök.

You might be wondering how you can pray to the god of light. While it is true that he's still in Hel, his new position there represents a poetic role: He is the light that can be found even in the darkest of places. If you call on him, he can give you peace and solace in times of strife. In times of darkness, he can cast light your way.

While you can verbally venerate him by way of prayer at an altar or by reciting verses of poetry venerating him, you can also give an offering to Baldur by being kind to someone in need, by helping someone who is stuck in the darkness. And once you have done that, you can light a candle in the dark and then recite his name to invoke his aid. He will see that you have been carrying on his legacy, and he will answer with his help.

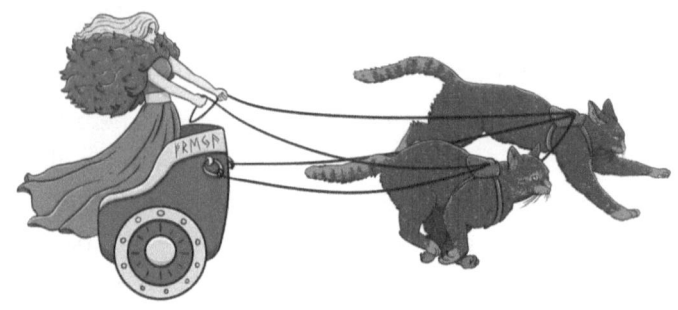

# F
reya — The Goddess of Fertility and Love

The goddess of fertility and love is more than just that. She is associated with magic, lust, sex, beauty, war, death, and gold. Her name, Freya, also pronounced as Freya, means "lady."

Although she is a Vanir goddess, she lives in Asgard with her husband, Odr. She has been made an honorary Æsir, called Asyunjur. After the Æsir and Vanir war, she was sent alongside her brother Frey and her father, Njord.

Freya's children, Hnoss and Gersemi, are known for their beauty. In the Prose Edda, there's a darker element to

Freya's tale as she constantly mourns her husband's disappearance. As to where he's gone, she does not know, but she goes out to find him while crying. Her tears fall into the sea and turn into amber.

She holds a monumental role in Norse mythology, given that it was she who taught the Æsir gods, including Odin, the magical known as seiðr. She was seen as a Völva in Norse mythology. A Völva is a seeress and sorceress who went from town to town, and in exchange for food and shelter, she would grant magic to those who helped her. It was because of her prowess in magic that she and her father were appointed as the high priests of sacrificial offerings.

When a warrior dies, it's not Odin who gets the first pick of whom to invite into the afterlife but Freya, who chooses half of the warriors for herself to stay with her in Fólkvangr while Odin gets the other half in Valhalla.

Her Völva persona was also granted credibility because of her love for travel. Her chariot that she used to travel on was one of a kind, being driven by two dark cats. She also had a cloak made from falcon feathers that allowed her to fly invisibly through the skies. Sometimes, she would loan the cloak to other gods and goddesses who needed to fly somewhere in a rush. The same cloak was borrowed by Loki to travel to the realm of the giants to rescue the goddess Iðunn. She also traveled using a boar named Hildsvini, whom Loki claimed was actually her human lover in disguise so that she could ride him in public. Many tales tell of Loki's spite towards Freya, one of them being his slanderous claim that she was bedding every single one of the gods and elves present in the halls during

Aegir's feast. Her father came to her side and said that Loki was utterly perverted for slandering her like that.

Her beauty was so famous among all the creatures in the realm that once a giant disguised himself and came to work as a mason, with his barter being Freya's hand in marriage if he were to build the wall within a year.

But then there are also stories of her promiscuousness present in the old fables, such as when she came upon a beautiful necklace being created by the dwarves, she asked to buy it, but when the dwarves said that the payment would not be in gold or precious stones but by sleeping with each of the dwarves, Freya agreed, sleeping with all four of them in exchange for the necklace.

She's been known to be a wild and free spirit, often reveling in parties and enjoying the pleasures of the flesh. That's how she is associated with fertility, not through agriculture but through her passion for lovemaking and conceiving children.

Praying to her and offering her sacrifices should be done with the utmost sincerity, as Freya cares about honesty, truth, and kindness. As she is the goddess of sexuality, you can make offerings such as honey, chocolate, bread, fresh fruits, and even poetry to her. Her role is not confined to being that of a fertility goddess. Freya has mastery of warcraft and can be considered a warrior goddess. You can offer feathers and bones as offerings, as this is symbolic of warcraft. Other offerings that you can place in honor of her include amber, amber incense, lavender, sunflowers, daisies, and ladybugs. When making offerings, leave them on a dedicated altar built just for Freya. On this altar, you can leave a picture of

Freya or an artistic depiction of her. Freya loved flowers, so add some flowers to the altar as well. If you want to delve further into her worship, consider learning the Futhark runes, as she was the master of these runes. They would even allow you to communicate directly with her. If you are inclined towards magic, you should learn and practice seiðr.

# Frey — The Splendid God of Fertility

Son of Njord and brother of Freya, Frey's name stands for "lord." Associated with things that bring fertility, such as sunshine, rain, harvest, and material prosperity, Frey lives in the land of the light elves, Alfheim, which he received as a present.

Frey had a ship that he was famous for. It was a ship so big it could fit all the gods inside it, yet, when it was folded, it became so tiny that it could fit inside a purse.

Once, Frey snuck upon Odin's throne and looked at the nine realms. And as he was musing and looking, he saw a woman that was so beautiful that he became immensely captivated by her. Her name was Gerd, the daughter of the giants Gymir and Aurboda. Frey was so occupied with her thoughts that he stopped eating and drinking altogether to the point of sickness.

This made his father, Njord, very worried. When he inquired through his servant Skirnir as to what was wrong with Frey, Frey responded that he was in love with Gerd. To help his condition, Skirnir went to Jötunheimr to try to bring Gerd to Asgard.

But Gerd was not seduced by the promise of immortality or jewels. A vexed Skrinir started to threaten her with curses and said he would use the secret knowledge of runes to make her life perilous. This scared her enough to come to Asgard and marry Frey. But she had a condition. She wanted to wait for nine days before coming to Asgard, primarily to torture the lovelorn Frey psychologically.

Here's a particularly strange part of this tale. Skirnir, when he went to the land of the giants, took Frey's magical sword with him to protect himself. Skirnir took this sword as the price for bringing Gerd. According to legend, this sword was capable of fighting on its own. And it was because he lost his sword that he would perish during Ragnarök.

But his perishing would be just as legendary as his life. He would face Surtr, the fire giant, and kill him in battle. But this battle would weigh heavy on him and take his life as well.

When making an offering to Frey, remember that he is the god of fertility both in terms of sexuality and in terms of farming. So, offer him things like grains, nuts, legumes, seeds, apples, baked bread, and if you're feeling particular, you can even offer him pork, as pigs are a form of livestock. In addition, you can offer him things that are phallic in nature, as he's the sexual god of fertility. Traditionally, people used to leave the last sheaf of wheat standing in their crops as an offering to Frey. His Nordic nature allows you to sacrifice alcoholic drinks like dark beers and apple cider to him as well. Ideal times to thank Frey and offer him sacrifices is when you get a lot of abundance and fertility in your life. Think along the lines of financial gain, becoming a parent to a healthy child, or finding love in your life. That's when you should thank Frey by way of making offerings.

# Heimdall — Protector of Asgard

With teeth fashioned out of gold, a tall physique, and beauty that rivals that of Frey and Baldur, Heimdall is the guardian god, protecting Asgard by guarding the Bifrost, the only way into the realm.

His birth must have been a strange occurrence as he had nine mothers. How he was born of nine mothers is a whimsical mystery unto itself.

He shone brightly and was considered the whitest of the gods. His unparalleled abilities made him the perfect choice to stand guard at the Bifrost. For instance, he slept less than a bird. He could see for thousands of miles in every direction, even in pure darkness. Such strong was his sight that he could observe blades of grass growing. He could also hear exceptionally well. It was said that he could hear the sound of wool growing on the back of a sheep.

He lived in a place called the Himinbjörg. When he was free from his duties, he liked to ride around on his horse named Gulltop. This horse was made entirely of gold, ergo the name "Gold top."

When he stood guard at the Bifrost, he had his sword, the Hǫfuð, to protect himself and to fight off any unwelcome people. For the direst of circumstances, when he needed to call upon the gods for help, he had a horn named Gjallarhorn. The gods would hear this horn upon the brink of Ragnarök, knowing that the end is near.

Like many other deities, Heimdall was Odin's son.

Heimdall had a fondness for human beings. For that very reason, he can be honored, venerated, worshipped, and offered sacrifices with relative simplicity. You can call on him with the purest of sincerity, and he will answer. To understand why you should bestow offerings unto him, it's important to know that he holds sway over several domains such as wisdom, purpose, focus, perception, commitment, protection, a familial bond, safety, communication, love, and devotion to one's duty.

Remember this when making an offering: He is sharp of sight and sees all that transpires, so approach him with honesty. Mead is an excellent offering to him. Coffee is as well. You should reflect upon Heimdall's purpose while meditating to understand his role and what he did, and how you can become a better person by being more watchful and careful in your life.

His is the domain of vigilance, so if you need more vigilance in your life, making a humble offering will do that for you. Pork, lamb, and mutton are excellent choices for offerings. In addition, anything caffeinated when offered will draw his favor to you. You can also guide others, help someone in need, and mentor someone who needs mentoring to honor Heimdall.

## Frigg — The Goddess of Marriage, Motherhood, and Fertility

Queen of the Æsir, wife of the All-father Odin, and mother to Baldur and Hodr, Frigg was one of the most powerful goddesses in the Norse pantheon. She knew seiðr magic which she could use to alter the tapestry of fate. Frigg represented family, devotion, love, patience, motherhood, and nurturing. We have already seen one of her displays of maternal love when she tried to undo Baldur's fate by pleading to all the beings in the universe not to harm her son.

In terms of symbology, she is represented by the sky, the moon, mistletoe, silver, and the spinning wheel and its spindle.

Her role as Odin's wife was a very influential position. She could make her husband do things that she wanted, and he, loving her devotedly, always complied. A few times, he was even tricked into making a decision, but he never resented her for it.

Frigg was not only the mother to her two sons but also the stepmother to Thor, Heimdall, Tyr, Bragi, Vidar, Vali, and Hermod.

She played things close to the chest. Despite possessing the gift of prophecy, she never revealed what she knew.

She was the only other being in Asgard permitted to sit on Odin's throne to look at the nine realms. Her abode was Fensalir, a hall surrounded by wet marshes.

Her maidens always surrounded her. One of them, Fulla, was very close to her to the point that Frigg shared her deepest secrets. Gná was yet another maiden who tended to all of Frigg's needs and was her loyal messenger. When Frigg had to intervene or protect someone or something, she would send her maiden Hlín to do this vital task.

Frigg was a force of goodness, always looking out for others and caring for the smallest of things.

The All-mother should be given offerings that suit her stature. She stands for motherhood, familial strength, and homeliness. When venerating her, you should consider the things she is associated with. In terms of food, you can offer her something that contains cardamom. She will also appreciate savory meals like stews, porridge, and roasts. In terms of drinks, think along the lines of white wine, plum wine, sake, and even milk. If you clean your house while meditating about Frigg, her bounties will fall upon you. Since her home is in the marshes, things such as feathers from marsh birds and pictures of the marshes are also excellent offerings.

# Hel — The Goddess of The Underworld

When a person dies from old age and illness or is considered too much of a coward or a dishonorable person unfit for the afterlife realms of Odin or Freya, they go to Helheim. And it is here Hel ruled. Daughter of Loki and a giantess named Angrboða, Hel's family extends to Fenrir, the wolf, and Jörmungandr, the world serpent.

Make no mistake, Hel is quite like the realm she rules over. She is ruthless, powerful, harsh, cruel, threatening, and filled with malignant malice. Norse mythology saw her as being very indifferent being completely unconcerned with the matters of living beings and the dead.

Her name does not imply any relation to the Christian concept of hell. Hel meant hidden, a word that also referred to those who had passed away, considering that they were hidden from the world of the living by way of being buried or cremated or that their souls were invisible to the living.

Descriptions of her were scarce in old texts, but the surviving texts described her as humanoid, half white and half blue.

Her trickery, which she notably got from her father, allowed her to hold Baldur in Helheim even though the gods wanted him back. It was said that she was thrown into Helheim by Odin who wanted to prevent the coming of Ragnarök for as long as possible. Once she was banished to this realm, she decided to crown herself queen and rule over this cold, dark, and desolate place.

Rather than fight her dark persona, she ultimately gave into it to the point where everything in her hall bore the name of some misfortune. Her dining table was known as hunger, and her knives were known as starvation. Her bed was called the sick bed, and the curtains in her room were named misfortune.

When dealing with the passing of a loved one, or when trying to overcome an existential crisis, especially within the context of death, you can turn to Hel and make an offering to her, venerating her for her role as the queen of the dead. If you're struggling with dark thoughts, depression, and mental anguish, you can also make an offering to her. Why? Imagine the mental fortitude and courage she must possess to thrive in a land as desolate and cold and devoid of light as Hel. She must possess a strong resolve, which in turn, she can grant you if you venerate her.

If you intend to propitiate Hel, attend funerals, visit the dead in graveyards, work on your mental health, offer help to those suffering from mental illnesses, or volunteer at a cemetery or a hospice program. You can also volunteer for roadkill cleanup and say a prayer for the spirit of the dead animals.

If you want a more traditional sort of veneration, then you can create an altar that contains animal fur, animal bones, skulls, horns, skeletons, black mirrors, black candles, wormwood, black roses, and grave rubbings. In terms of drinks, resonate with Hel by making a cup of black tea or black coffee. Apples can serve as an offering, too, as Hel has an apple orchard that she's quite fond of.

But most importantly, live your life to the fullest. It sounds like simple advice, but the truth is Hel appreciates those who don't live a half-dead, half-alive life. If you devote yourself to living fully, you will be ready for it when your time comes to die.

# Loki — The Trickster

Before Tom Hiddleston donned his green robes for Marvel's Thor and Neil Gaiman portrayed him as Low Key Lyesmith in American Gods, Loki was not seen as a charming or swoon-worthy god, but rather a cunning god of mischief and trickery. The Poetic Edda dubbed him "the contriver of fraud."

He was the son of Farbauti and Laufey. While Laufey was an Æsir goddess, Farbauti was a jötunn. He was associated with the Æsir from his mother's side. And that's why he took the surname of Laufeyson when residing in Asgard.

You must not think him entirely evil. Mischief and trickery are different from evil. Sometimes, Loki used his trickery to help the Æsir gods, such as when he seduced a horse to hinder the efforts of a giant who wanted to make the walls of Asgard within a year to win Freya's hand. But his trickery was ambiguous, as he also used his cunning to send Baldur to Hel.

He was a chaotic character. That much can be said for certain. Once, when he was about to get killed by the giant Thiazi, Loki bartered his life by bringing him the goddess of immortality, Iðunn. And now that he had handed over Iðunn to Thiazi, the gods threatened him with death unless he brought her back. It was originally his mistake that Iðunn was captured by Thiazi. But he set matters straight when he went back to save her by shifting into a falcon and carrying Iðunn back to Asgard in his talons. Thiazi pursued Loki but was killed off by the gods when they burned him to death.

Rather than end here, the matter devolved into further chaos when Skaði, Thiazi's daughter, came for restitution, asking for revenge for her father's death. She demanded that the gods make her laugh, a feat that only Loki succeeded in doing by tying his testicles with a rope to a goat's beard. When the goat tugged, Loki writhed in pain. This spectacle was so absurd and hilarious that Skaði began laughing.

After the horrendous events resulting in the death of Baldur, the gods tied Loki to chains in Muspelheim. They placed a venomous serpent over his head, forever to remain there until Ragnarök.

Upon Ragnarök, Loki will break free and fight alongside the giants against the gods in the last great battle.

Loki will take on Heimdall, and the two shall fight each other until their death.

One can argue that it was Loki's chaotic effect throughout Norse mythology that will eventually cause Ragnarök. His three children, Jörmungandr, Hel, and Fenrir, whom he had with the jötunn Angrboða, became elemental forces capable of wreaking unimaginable amounts of havoc. Odin took drastic measures and threw Hel into Helheim, cast Jörmungandr in Midgard's sea, and restrained Fenrir within Asgard—all in an attempt to put off Ragnarök as long as he could. Odin knew the prophecies and knew that these three characters would cause Ragnarök. And in the end, he was right Loki, Jörmungandr, Hel, Fenrir, and Surtr will serve as the antagonistic forces causing Ragnarök.

But here is the paradox that will leave you undecided about Loki, despite his chaos, despite his plotting the murder of Baldur, despite his imprisonment: Odin referred to Loki as his brother, calling him the blood of his own blood. Thor often chose Loki as a traveling companion. Many gods and goddesses took his counsel, paying heed to his twisted wisdom. He was a force to be reckoned with.

He had a high standard for entertainment. His mischief was often to serve as his own amusement. And mischief was not his only domain. He knew different kinds of magic and was exceptionally skilled in shapeshifting. He had mastered the art of shifting into any living creature he wanted.

You can offer him meats, curries, and spicy foods at an altar. Additionally, foods that contain tons of sugar, such as cupcakes, brownies, candies, and chocolates, are bound to attract his attention. Loki drank alongside Odin. Whenever Odin drank, so did Loki. So, offering him strong alcohol, coffee, drinks with full-fat content, and anything delectable.

If you want to venerate him through your actions, then think about creating mischief. Don't do anything too drastic that will get you in trouble with the police or anything. Think stand-up comedy at the local Laugh Factory or practical jokes on your friends. Loki also has a whimsical side that appreciates novelty toys and puzzles, so that might be a great offering if you want to appeal to his fun side.

# N jord — God of the Wind and the Seas

Njord, the Vanir god of the seas, ships, fishing, hunting, and the wind, was also associated with wealth, peace, prosperity, and fertility. After the Æsir and Vanir war, he came to live in Asgard with his two children, Frey and Freya. He made Nóatún his dwelling beside the sea, as this was a calm and quiet place where he could look at the sea, listen to its waves, and enjoy the salty wind coming from the windows of his home.

The surviving stories about Njord tell a sad tale of an unhappy marriage with Skaði. After the killing of Thiazi,

Skaði came seeking revenge but decided to reconcile in exchange for a few favors, one of whom was the gods making her laugh. The other was a far more serious proposition. She wanted to be married to a husband of her choosing. The giant was asked to choose her husband by looking at their feet, as their bodies were hidden behind a veil. Thinking that she had chosen Baldur, she mistakenly selected Njord.

The two were married, but this life was not a happy life for either of them. They started fighting right after marriage about where they would live. Skaði wanted to live in the high mountainous lands of her father's homeland, while Njord wanted to live alongside the sea. They came to a compromise, deciding to live for some days in Thrymheimr and some days by the sea. But despite this compromise, they complained to each other about each other's choice of dwelling.

They grew apart eventually, Skaði returning to the mountains and Njord returning to the seaside. Njord then had children with his sister, a common thing for the Vanir gods.

At the end of Ragnarök, Njord will survive and return to the Vanir.

Despite his troublesome life, Njord was a very generous god. In terms of offerings, when you offer him food, make sure it's seafood, as he loves things such as clam chowders, herring, rye crackers, and fried fish. Any food made in the shape of seashells will do just as fine as well. You can also offer him strong liquor, dark beer, vodka, and gin. Material offerings include seashells, spices, and things that can be used as currency, such as gold, beads, and stones.

He also has a fondness for tobacco, fishing gear, boats, and anchors. A miniature ship—such as a ship in a bottle—would be a thoughtful offering.

# Odin — The All-Father, Ruler of The Gods

So much can be said about the most powerful god in Norse mythology. Words fall short of his magnificence. His wisdom is unmatched. His powers extend into the disciplines of wisdom, royalty, death, healing, poetry, the runes, magic, creation, diplomacy, and shape-shifting. Considered the leader of souls, both mortal and immortal, Odin truly personifies the monumentalism that befits Norse mythology.

You can trace his lineage back to creation itself. The grandson of the first Æsir, Búri, Odin was the son of Borr and the half-giant Bestla. He had two brothers, Vili and Ve. Together, these brothers created the world. Odin was married to Frigg, with whom he had Baldur and Hodr. Odin often visited Jötunheimr and was swept away by the beauty of the women living there. With them, he had sons, including Thor and Vali.

He was able to morph into the shape of any human or animal whenever he wanted. He would wander about wearing different guises, such as the guise of an old, cane-bearing, bearded man, listening to the matters of the world.

When he spoke, it was with such a soft and gentle voice that all who heard him believed that he was always telling the truth. It just was that he always spoke in rhyme and riddles. But his words possessed deep magic. With a single utterance of a brief word, he could make fire erupt from nothingness. With a gentle assurance, he could calm down the sea. His ability to speak entirely in poetry came from drinking the mead of poetry, which he stole from the giants. At certain times, he granted the gods favor by allowing them to drink from this mead.

An interesting fact here is that the drink's name is Óðrœrir, which means "the stirrer of Óðr." Óðr refers to ecstasy or inspiration. This is also the origin of Odin's name.

He was not a complacent god, although that was not his first nature. But whenever he did take part in a battle, he wounded his enemies to the point of blindness, deafness, or leaving them horrorstruck upon witnessing Odin's war visage. Furthermore, Odin had the power to infuse his men with powers to make them strong as bears and berserk with bloodlust. In his hands, ordinary items such as sticks or twigs turned into dangerous weapons.

Some of his powers came with grave weight. He could see the future and past of all beings. This meant that he knew of Ragnarök and knew there was nothing he could do to prevent its arrival. Yet still, he took some measures to ensure that it would be delayed.

One of his powers was the ability to travel to far-off lands and the ability to travel through other people's memories.

As he was the most powerful of gods, his thought was his will, and his will was absolute. He could kill someone or inflict them with a fatal illness just by thinking of it. The strongest of the Norse folk, the Vikings, offered him sacrifices to earn his favor in battle. People also made human sacrifices to him, especially by slaying their enemies in war. Sometimes, the sacrifice would involve spearing someone or tying them to a noose or even both at the same time. In combat, Odin's believers used to fling their spears while crying, "Odin owns ye all!"

Odin was also noted to have the power to communicate with the dead. He was even able to raise them from the dead.

Courtesy of Loki, Odin had the eight-legged horse Sleipnir as his steed. This magical horse was not only capable of crossing long distances in record time but it was fascinating in its appearance, beautiful to all who laid eyes upon it. It could travel in the air just as well as on land. Loki gifting Odin Sleipnir could be seen as a symbol of the bond that existed between these two gods.

Two ravens named Huginn (Thought) and Muninn (Memory) were a spiritual extension of Odin. He would send them out into the world to bring him news from all the realms. They would come to him in the evening and whisper what they saw and heard. When idle, these ravens sat beside Odin on his throne.

Odin also had two wolves named Geri (the hungry one) and Freki (the greedy one) as his loyal pets. These wolves would walk with him when he walked in the avenues of Asgard. Odin didn't need food to survive, so whenever food was placed in front of him on the table, he gave it to his wolves. He preferred drinking wine, anyways.

Among his most renowned weapons was the spear Gungnir, made from Yggdrasil itself. Odin carved runes onto his spear, imbuing it with magic, making it always hit its mark and kill his opponents.

He wore a ring known as Draupnir, out of which new rings dripped out every eighth or ninth day. This ring was given to him by the dwarves Brokkr and Eitri.

One of his most notable feats is the sacrifice of his eye as payment for drinking from Mimir's well. Odin became the wisest of all gods after drinking from the well, gaining all of Mimir's wisdom.

His quest for wisdom and knowledge did not stop there. He wanted to understand runes and learn their secrets. This could only be done through the ultimate sacrifice. So he pierced himself with his spear and hung himself from

Yggdrasil for nine days and nights. When he eventually fell from Yggdrasil, the meaning of the runes was revealed to him.

When you consider making sacrifices or offerings to Odin, remember that he's the god of sacrifices, whether it was losing his eye or hanging from the world tree. Self-sacrifice was sort of his thing. With that in mind, when you decide to offer something to the god of all gods, make sure it's something that you hold in high regard, something that's dear to you.

Create an altar space and devote it to Odin. If you are a practitioner of Wicca or tarot, place the Hanged Man card on that altar, as well as runes, raven feathers, horseshoes, a representation of a wolf, and beer/mead.

When offering food, place foods that look like spears onto the altar. Garlic, leeks, cucumbers, asparagus, and so forth. You can also place beef, meat, pork roast, and steak as a food offering.

In terms of drink, Odin loves to drink. So red wine, mead, dark-colored alcohol like whiskey—anything along those lines would be a well-suited offering.

Odin loves poetry. You can write some of your poetry, venerating him, and ask for his help in your daily life. If you learn runes, praying to him will be easier, as he is also the god of runes.

In life, if you want Odin's favor, you must also pursue knowledge with the same relentlessness and fervor that Odin displayed in his life. As Odin once slayed monsters, so should you strive to slay metaphorical monsters that plague our world. Things like racism, homophobia, and sexism are some of the metaphorical monsters that you can fight to venerate Odin.

# Thor — the God Of Thunder

The almighty god of thunder, Odinson, one of the most powerful of the Norse gods, ally to humans, Thor ruled over strength, lightning, thunder, oak trees, and bravery. He was considered extremely strong—arguably the strongest. However, he was not extremely wise or clever, unlike Loki or Freya, or Odin. To that effect, some of the giants teased him for his brawn-over-brains disposition.

Oh, yes, the giants loved to make fun of Thor because Thor was, let's put it mildly, quick to anger, allowing his rage to take control of him. And when Thor became furious, lightning issued from him, thunderclouds gathered over him, and he swung his hammer, hitting the giants in their heads. The sound of thunder drove fear into the hearts of the giants. Some would even go so far as to say Thor welcomed it when the giants teased him because it allowed him to go toe to toe with them.

Unlike what Marvel tells us, Thor did not marry Dr. Jane Foster. Instead, he married another goddess named Sif, and together they had Trud and Modi. Thor's house Thrúdheim was the biggest in all of Asgard. Thor also adopted a stepson named Ullr. Thor sired a son with the giantess Jarnsaxa. This son's name was Magni.

Particularly famous in Norse lore and modern adaptations are Thor's goats who drew his chariot. As Thor flew across the sky, the sound of the wheels and the sparks emitting from his chariot made people aware that Thor was flying over them. The funny thing about the goats, whenever Thor visited some far-off land, he used to slay the goats to eat them. Then, when he reached home, he revived them with his hammer.

Speaking of his hammer, the dwarves Eitri and Brokkr made a weapon one of its kind, a frightening armament capable of throwing out lightning bolts and holding enough power and magic within itself to tear down entire mountains. It also had auto-aim, allowing it to hit any target from any distance. This hammer was called Mjölnir.

Once Thor hit someone with Mjölnir, the hammer would return itself to Thor's hand. Mjölnir was not only capable of destruction but of bringing life to the dead as well. It could revive animals and humans alike. Also, it could make itself small enough to fit inside Thor's clothes.

Combined with his magical belt and gauntlets, the hammer made him extremely strong.

A famous tale regarding Thor is about him losing his beloved hammer. A giant Thrym stole his hammer and hid it within the recesses of the earth. Thor was quite a temperamental god; without his hammer, he was furious. So, Loki, normally very mischievous and sly, decided to help Thor out. Thrym told him that he would return the hammer in exchange for Freya's hand in marriage.

Freya, of course, said no. In her anger at this boisterous appeal, she became so furious that the entire Asgard shook to its core.

The gods decided to think up an alternate solution. Heimdall proposed that they should deceive the giant, but how? He suggested Thor wear a wedding dress, wear Freya's necklace, and go instead of her. Thor became extremely angry over this, but somehow the gods managed to convince him, and Loki joined in, deciding to accompany Thor as his bridesmaid.

When they arrived in Jötunheimr, the giant Thrym was surprised when he saw that "Freya" devoured an entire ox, eight salmon, and a complete barrel of mead during the feast. Loki explained, saying that "Freya" had not eaten in eight days in anticipation of her marriage, thus the hunger.

When Thrym decided to kiss "Freya," he recoiled in shock at her manly features. Loki said this was because she had been starving for eight nights.

Mjölnir was taken out from its hidden place and placed on the bride's lap as a customary gift. And that's when Thor decided to get rid of his drag persona and reveal himself. He crushed the skulls of all the giants present there with Mjölnir and returned with his hammer back to Asgard.

Thor was quite fond of humans and spent much time on Midgard. You could say that he was the god of the common man. This makes him less specific in terms of offerings than other gods, especially Odin.

In terms of food, whatever you offer, make sure it is in large quantities. Salmon, pork, beef, lamb, pickled herring, whatever you can think of. As I said, he's not very particular about what it is as much as he is about how much of it there is.

Dark beers, ales, meads, and stout should be offered as drinks.

You should consider offering him tools and hammers when offering him an item. Blacksmithing tools, any tools that come under the jurisdiction of manual labor, and even ornamental weaponry. If you can find something that's been struck by lightning, such as tree bark, you can offer that to him as well.

Remember that he was the god of common folk. He was very concerned with how humans lived their lives and if they were well or not. If you devote your time to the community and help out those in need, you will be venerating Thor in your everyday life.

# Tyr — The Warrior God

The actual god of war in Norse mythology was not Kratos, despite what the PlayStation game might have you believe. Instead, it was Tyr, the lawgiver, the warrior, the bravest of the gods, and the binder of Fenrir. Once, he was even the leader of the gods of the Norse pantheon but was replaced by Odin.

Tyr was concerned with justice, especially justice in the field of battle. He was extremely fair and just in all the treaties he made.

A particularly well-known tale of his bravery included his binding Fenrir. All the gods were too afraid to approach Fenrir, but Tyr bravely decided to pacify the great wolf by putting his hand in the wolf's mouth while the gods bound him to a rock. When Fenrir noticed that this was a trick, he became angry and tore off Tyr's right hand.

As brave as this sacrifice was, this served as Tyr's downfall. His role became less important in the eyes of the gods as he was not at full strength. Once, when Tyr tried to defend Frey from Loki's insults, Loki snidely said that Tyr couldn't be the right hand of justice. Other gods, while they were not as cruel as Loki, also saw him as weakened and less worthy of overseeing his role as a god of war, law, and justice.

And his final fall will come at Ragnarök, when he will fight—ironically enough—another giant creature, a dog named Garm, who is the guardian of Hel. Tyr will defeat him singlehandedly but will also perish in this fight.

When considering offering something to Tyr, remember that he, like Odin, was a god familiar with sacrifice, as he gave away his right hand in the name of bravery. He was brave and honorable, despite the lack of his right hand. You can offer beef, pork, strong wine, and dark ale as foods to Tyr, and in terms of general offerings, you can choose the path of righteousness, honor, and bravery in your daily life. When you make a promise, make sure to keep it.

Followers of Asatru, who use altars as an extension of their veneration and offerings, can place an ornamental sword on the altar, decorate the altar with red and grey colors, and inscribe Tyr's rune on the altar items.

# B ragi — The God of Poetry

Son of Odin, the god of poetry and music, Bragi was known for his wisdom, creativity, and knowledge of songs and poetry. The word Bragi means poet/poetry.

Bragi had runes carved on his tongue, presumably to enhance his eloquence. He was the husband of Iðunn, the goddess of youth and immortality. Bragi was depicted with a harp, which was a testament to his musical prowess and melodic nature.

His beautiful singing voice was second to none, and when he played the harp, the sound was nothing short of holy. Gods tried to keep him around so that he would delight and charm them.

Bragi had a central role in Asgard. He would welcome the fallen warriors into Valhalla and greet them with poetry and music.

In our modern life, it is important to remember that without entertainment in the form of music, songs, and arts, life would be extremely monotonous. Almost everyone listens to music. The gift of music and poetry makes the world much more alive. We should all be thankful to Bragi for it. In terms of food and drink, you can offer him anything that you would offer a welcomed guest in your house. As music and drinking go hand in hand (as do drinking and poetry), why not offer him a nice wine, whiskey, or beer? But it is not in food or drink that you should look for offerings to Bragi.

It is in music.

If you make an altar, place musical instruments on top of it, books of classical poetry, scores of music, runes specific to Bragi, and anything related to music or poetry.

If you want to offer your services to Bragi, think of all the indie musicians out there, the starving artists trying to survive in a world filled with record labels and corporatized music. You can support a musician by donating to them or buying their album, taking an eager person to a concert, visiting a musical show, contributing to a charity for musicians and performing arts, and giving money to street musicians when you come across them. That's how you honor Bragi.

If you are well-versed in poetry and are a bit of a poet yourself, you can write some poetry and offer it to Bragi, venerating him and his essence. Make sure it's a good poem, though. You're presenting your work to the god of poetry. It kind of sets the bar high. This should also be kept in mind when offering Bragi any story or song.

We have covered several of the notable gods in this chapter, and as we progress in our understanding of Norse mythology and Norse Paganism, we will also uncover other gods. We will also learn how to make offerings to the gods when we learn about modern pagan practices and belief systems such as Asatru.

The world of Norse mythology was rich in beings and creatures other than gods, goddesses, giants, and elves. In the next chapter, we'll take a deep dive into the various mystical, fantastical creatures that dwelled in the nine realms.

# CHAPTER 6
# THE CREATURES OF NORSE MYTHOLOGY

In today's age of skepticism, it has hard to find wonderment when one looks around. The minute a kid turns into an adolescent, it's been brought to their knowledge that it was mommy and daddy who left the cookies and presents out on Christmas night and that Santa never existed. As their imagination suffers a severe blow, children have to come to terms with the fact that the Tooth Fairy, the Easter Bunny, and likewise so many other characters featured on the roster of their daydreams, and unbridled imagination start coming out as less-than-real. They come to terms with a reality where mystical creatures and fantastical figures do not exist outside the confines of entertainment.

Back in the age of wonder, this was not the case. Put yourself in the leather shoes of a Viking sailing in their longship and imagine what the world would have appeared from his perspective. Below him, in the sea, the great world serpent lay sleeping. Were this Viking to dive deep enough, he might come face-to-face with Jörmungandr himself. When he looked to the mountains, he knew as certain as day that those were the vestiges of Ymir. Those two crows flying across the sky could be Odin's ravens, Huginn and Muninn. Perhaps the All-Father favored this Viking and was keeping an eye on him. Fear took the Viking's heart as his ship lurched and bobbed against the waves. Was it possible that the infernal Kraken was below him, twisting its tentacles, waiting to attack?

"All-Father, protect me," He would supplicate.

And then, the dark sky would light up with lightning. Thunder would roar, and blue streaks would etch across the canopy of clouds, bolstering the spirit of this Viking and his fellow seamen. For as long as the ally of the people of Midgard, Thor, was on their side, no Kraken nor sea serpent could harm them.

At nightfall, the Viking would look to the skies, looking at the stars, wondering about the fiery depths of Muspelheim from where these embers came. Upon hearing the howl of a wolf at full moon's night, he would wonder if Ragnarök was near and if Fenrir had broken free from his chains.

By every definition, this old world was a magical world populated with mythical creatures. Almost all high fantasy novels, games, and movies have taken inspiration from the creatures mentioned in Norse mythology, from the elves, dwarves, and dragons in Lord of the Rings to the gargantuan Kraken in Pirates of the Caribbean, the influence of Norse mythology is still there.

We could all reignite that magic in our lives and find joy in believing again, just as the Norse did once and just as we did when we were little, and the world was still a place of wonder.

Let's look at Norse mythology's diverse ecosystem and populate our bestiaries with the creatures who thrived in the Nine Realms.

**Elves**

Long before Legolas, Elrond, and Galadriel existed in Tolkien's legendarium, the elves of Alfheim drove awe in the hearts of the Norse people. Described as more vibrant in their beauty than the sun itself, the elves were known to have an ethereal appearance.

While they were not considered as omnipotent in terms of godhood as the Vanir and Æsir, it was largely believed that the elves were powerful nonetheless, capable of making humans fall ill, controlling nature, holding sway over fertility, and using their divine magical knowledge for curing ailments.

In the Poetic Edda, Snorri Sturluson divided the elves into two categories: the light elves and the dark elves, the former residing in Alfheim while the latter, thought to be dwarves, living underground in Svartalfheim.

Before and during the Viking Age, people worshipped the elves and even hosted ceremonies in their honor, including one called Álfablót, which many modern-day Asatru communities still hold today.

According to lore, humans and elves could marry each other and produce offspring that resembled humans but had the magical abilities of elves. It might also be possible that humans could transcend and become elves after their death.

## Huldra

Scandinavian folklore tells us a tale that would put the fear of Odin in the hearts of young single men everywhere. The Huldra was a gorgeous, elf-like female creature with flowing locks of long blonde hair. Donning a floral crown, this spirit lurked in the forest, looking for young men to marry.

You might be thinking that this creature doesn't sound half-bad. She's pretty, she's a maiden, and all she wants is to get married. Well, the tip-off might be the cow tail that she had. Most men fled in terror when they saw her, identifying her from that strange tail jutting out of her rear.

But what would happen if she caught up with you? She would trap you in the mountains until you finally gave in and agreed to marry her. If you refused to marry her, she would kill you. But you would be doomed regardless, for if you married her in a church or a temple in the name of god, her tail would disappear, and she would morph into the most hideous looking woman ever, gaining the strength of ten men. She'd then proceed to kill you, anyway.

## Fenrir

It makes poetic sense that the harbinger of Ragnarök happens to be the child of Loki. Loki mated with Angrboða to produce three particularly quintessential offspring: the goddess of the underworld, Hel; the great serpent, Jörmungandr; and the humongous wolf, Fenrir. You might sympathize with him for a bit. As he grew older, the wolf kept growing in size, unable to control his stature. He grew so large that his gaping mouth was large enough to extend across the skies. Only Tyr was brave enough to approach and be friendly with the wolf. In time, he grew to the size of the apocalyptic beast that was prophesied to kill Odin.

Odin knew this and knew that there was no way to prevent this. But through his wisdom, he knew that he could delay the inevitable with extreme preparedness.

The first two times that the gods tried to tie down Fenrir, they failed. He'd break free from the fetters without breaking a sweat. But in their desperation, the gods went to the dwarves. The dwarves knew that this was an impossible task. So they crafted the constraints out of impossible things such as the spit of birds, beards of women, roots of mountains, the breath of fishes, stomping of cats, and the nervousness of bear. From this amalgam was created Gleipnir, a fetter that Tyr used to bind Fenrir. Then, for good measure, they pried his mouth open with a sword. Fenrir howled in pain and agony, his saliva dripping down and creating a river called "Anticipation/Expectation."

During Ragnarök, he will break free and kill Odin, devouring his body.

### The Kraken

A great horror haunted the depths of the seas. This oceanic beast was larger than life. Large enough to be misperceived as an island. Were anyone to step foot on this "island," they would perish into the gaping maw of the fearsome Kraken.

When it would rise to the surface of the sea to devour ships, the Kraken would cause maelstroms and whirlpools. Sometimes, though, the Kraken opted for a pescatarian diet. It lured fish towards itself by secreting thick excrement that attracted fish from all over the area.

With large tentacles and a cephalopodic face that was huge enough to devour entire ships, could this mythical beast have been the ancestor of squids and octopuses? Or was it the other way around? Were squids and octopuses the inspiration for this creature?

In either case, the Kraken lives on in myth, whether in the form of Lovecraft's Cthulhu or in its original form in Pirates of the Caribbean.

**The Mare**

A wicked creature crawled atop people's chests as they slept, imbuing their dreams with horrors and paralyzing them in a state of fearful slumber. This is indeed where the word nightmare originates from.

While some believe that the mare was the embodiment of the souls of living people that left their bodies at night, others thought the mares to be malicious witches who could shape-shift into the form of animals when they were astral projecting.

A mare would touch a tree and cause its branches to entangle. It would touch a person and cause their hair to tie into knots.

The origins of this oppressive demonic spirit come from a saga written by Snorri Sturluson, in which he describes how King Vanlandi of Uppsala died at the hands of a mare.

It was said that when the king abandoned his wife, she became scorned and approached the Finnish sorceress Huld, asking her to exact vengeance. A bewitched king Vanlandi wanted to go to Finland, where his wife was. But the people around him insisted that he had fallen prey to witchcraft. Then the king suddenly became very sleepy and excused himself to his sleeping chambers. As he slept, he started moaning that the mare was upon him.

When his men broke into the room, they found the hideous creature sitting on him. She stood atop his legs when they tried to get her off his head. When they went to the legs, she raced back to the head. Through all this, the king was in utter agony. At long last, unable to take the suffering any longer, he died a painful death. This story accomplishes two things: It introduces us to a mythical creature while imparting the moral that one should never scorn their wife to the point of desperation.

### Jörmungandr

The only thing preventing Ragnarök from happening is the Jörmungandr holding his tail in his mouth. The moment he releases his tail, Ragnarök will start. As he thrashes, he will cause the earth to shake. These earthquakes will also allow Fenrir to break free from his chains. Loki will also be set free as a result of this commotion. But what would prompt him to release his tail and come to the surface, causing earthquakes?

It is said that Ragnarök will be preceded by winters so cold that they will turn the seas cold. This icy water will make Jörmungandr extremely uncomfortable, beckoning him to thrash and cause chaos.

And then, as we read in the section about Thor, there will be a legendary fight between the Midgard serpent and the god of thunder. Thor will kill the serpent, but not before getting imbued with venom. Then, Thor will look around the battlefield and see that Odin is having trouble in his battle with Fenrir. He will go try to approach his father to help him but will only take nine steps before falling and dying because of the venom.

### Auðumbla

If Odin, Vili, and Ve could be considered the patriarchal figures who took it upon themselves to create the world, Auðumbla, the primeval cow, could be viewed as the original matriarch. Her maternal nature allowed her to feed Ymir and the rest of Ymir's children from her milk. She did not want for much, only the salty rime on the surface of the ice.

If she had not licked away at the ice, Búri, the first of the Æsir gods, would have never been freed from the ice. In that way, she can be considered the primordial matriarch to the gods.

### Níðhöggr

A dragon-like creature with deadly claws, a huge wingspan covered in scales, and rearing a horned head, this beast stayed at the root of the World Tree, gnawing away at its roots. He would chew on the bodies of the adulterers, murderers, thieves, and oath-breakers after they'd been banished to the shore of corpses, a location in the underworld reserved for criminals.

Níðhöggr hated the eagle who sat atop Yggdrasil and exchanged insults with it with the help of a squirrel. It is said that one day, one of these messages from the eagle will offend him so much that he'll shake himself free from the roots that have trapped him in the underworld, causing quakes across all Nine Realms. Once freed, the dragon will assist the giants in their fight with the gods.

To put this creature's size into perspective, think about how big the World Tree is. It nestles all Nine Realms on it. The World Tree is the cosmos itself. Níðhöggr is literally devouring the cosmos by gnawing the roots of Yggdrasil.

### Ratatoskr

According to one particular account, this tiny, mythical squirrel might as well have been the cause of Ragnarök. So vile and filled with maliciousness, this squirrel wanted to bring about the death of the tree of life. But he wasn't strong enough or big enough to do that. But he looked to the top of the tree and saw the eagle. Then, he looked below to the roots and saw Níðhöggr.

A scheme formed in his mind. He decided to fuel spite between these two creatures by passing on insults from one to the other, sometimes making up even worse insults and adding embellishments for maximum emotional damage. One day, he will insult Níðhöggr to such an extent that Níðhöggr will break free from the roots, disrupting the tree, and will join the giants in the fight against the gods. Some accounts go so far as to claim that Níðhöggr will cause the tree to collapse and will even kill the eagle sitting atop it, all because he was so offended by what Ratatoskr had said to him.

## Huginn and Muninn

The messengers of Odin, these two ravens acted as his eyes and ears. They would fly around the world and then return to their master to bring him vital information. They would sit on his shoulder whenever they'd return from their trips and caw everything they'd seen.

Odin held both these ravens in the highest of regards, paying more attention to what they had to say than his court subjects. In modern interpretations, the ravens symbolize Odin's knowledge and omniscience.

The Ravens were worshipped by the Nordic people and were depicted alongside Odin on numerous artifacts.

## Norns

The three Norns controlled the fate of all gods, mortals, and living things. They decided what would happen, when, and how. Wyrd, one of the Norns, represented the past. Verdandi represented the present. Skuld represented the future.

The Norns had one more important role; they were caretakers of Yggdrasil. To keep it from dying, the Norns fed it water from the well of Urd and poured it over its branches.

The Norns appear at a child's birth and decide how long he'll live, what he'll be fated to do, and whether he'll live a good or bad life. They then weave a thread of life and designate it to the child.

## Sleipnir

Despite the dubious circumstances in which this eight-legged steed was born, he became a figure of myth as Odin took a liking to it and deemed it worthy of being his steed. This horse was deemed the best horse among gods and men.

Svaldifari was an abnormally fast belonging to a giant who claimed that with Svaldifari's aid, he could build the borders around Asgard in less than a year. In exchange, the giant wanted to marry Freya. However, after taking Loki's word for it, the gods accepted the challenge. But as the giant progressed, it soon became clear that the wall would be built in less than a year.

So, Loki took one for the team, seducing Svaldifari by turning into a mare. The two horses raced around all night, putting a stop to the giant's work. Thus, the giant lost his wager. Loki had successfully seduced Svaldifari, but at what cost?

Well, Loki, in his mare form, became pregnant and gave birth months later to a foal with eight legs. Thus Sleipnir was the only creature in Norse myth born from two fathers.

Sleipnir was extremely beautiful, and Odin was so fond of him that he always took great care of him. Whenever Odin rode to war, he chose Sleipnir as his steed.

### Trolls

Two kinds of trolls populated the Nordic land and mythology. One was the giant, ugly troll that dwelled in mountains, forests, and dark places such as under bridges. And then there were the smaller trolls who looked like garden gnomes or sprites. These lived underground.

Regardless of their hideous appearance, they were creatures of fantasy, possessing magical powers that included prophecy. They weren't the brightest of creatures, often seen as quite hostile towards humans who crossed their paths.

Trolls were not able to come into sunlight. Whenever they came into contact with sunlight, they turned into stone. Some suggest that the Scandinavian countryside, which is so rocky and littered with large boulders, is a testament to the existence of trolls who got caught in sunlight.

As far as their appetites are concerned, they can eat almost anything, ranging from rocks in caves to small humans. Sometimes, they'd devour live goats in one gulp, as these were their favorite cuisine.

**Valkyrie**

These brave, beautiful, fierce women, riding winged steeds, were chosen by Odin to serve a glorious purpose. They were chosen to escort fallen warriors who had died honorably in a battle to their eternal abode, Valhalla.

They were described as hypnotizingly beautiful, delicate maidens with flaxen hair and porcelain skin. But their traits did not just extend to their beauty or their role on the battlefield as escorts. They were also tasked with choosing who would live or die in a battle. They could even use their powers to ascertain who would live and die.

No alive human is allowed to see them or be intimate with them. Sometimes, when the Valkyries are not overseeing battlegrounds, they are allowed to travel to different realms in the guise of a swan. If someone were to see them without their guise, the Valkyries would turn into a mortal and would be unable to return to Valhalla.

But in Valhalla, they do spend time with the fallen warriors, freely serving them food and drinks. They'd fill horns full of mead from a cauldron in Valhalla that kept being filled with endless mead from an enchanted goat named Heiðrún.

## Draugr

The term draugr means "someone who walks after death." The singular term is draugr, while the plural term is draugar. They're the Nordic equivalent of ghosts and zombies. They are, without a doubt, horrible creatures, carrying the unmistakable smell of decay wherever they go. Draugars are undead corpses that can not only move through rocks, thus explaining how they were able to escape their tombs and graves but also possess superhuman strength and can grow larger.

They serve many different purposes, including guarding their treasures, haunting living human beings, or torturing those who had tormented them in their life.

If they wished to kill a human, the draugars would crush them through their enlarged bodies, eat them whole, rip apart their bodies, and drink their blood. But this was not the worst thing they did. The most terrible ability a draugr possessed was the power to turn any sane person mad. They would drive living people insane, causing them to die out of hysteria or suicide.

How does one kill something already dead? The draugar could be killed if their bodies were dismembered or burned.

Some lore suggests that people believed that if someone was evil, malicious, unpopular, or simply vile, they would turn into a draugr after they died.

Have you picked on a pattern in this chapter? Did you understand how several of the creatures mentioned were intricately linked to life and death? From the Norns that controlled the fates of all beings to the Valkyries that welcomed fallen warriors into Valhalla, many creatures played a significant role in the life of an average Nordic person. Some were seen as cautionary tales as well. If you were a bad person in life, there were chances that you could either get reincarnated as a draugr or get sent to the depths of the underworld where Níðhöggr would devour your body.

More importantly, several of these creatures highlight the inevitability of death, teaching us that it is wise to come to terms with the reality of passing from one world to the other. If a being like Fenrir can devour the greatest god of all time, Odin, and if Jörmungandr's venom can kill someone as brave as Thor, we are but mere mortals. Rather than fear death or cower from it, we should aspire to experience a life well-lived, and when it's our time to die, we will have accepted that death is just as much a part of life as birth, adolescence, youth, and old age.

This gives us a perfect opportunity to understand the nature of death and the afterlife in Norse Paganism.

# CHAPTER 7
# THE AFTERLIFE

W hat happens to a person after they die? Is there such a thing as a soul, and if so, where does it go after the mortal vessel has perished? Is death something to be feared and delayed, or is it something akin to a long-lost friend to be greeted at the end of one's life?

Why do we talk of death in the first place? Is it because it's a philosophical black hole in the face of which all logic, planning, thinking, and preparing fail? Is it because beyond death lies complete uncertainty and unknowing that we're so afraid of it? Are we afraid of not existing any longer? Or worse, if we still exist after death, are we afraid of existing in polarized states—that of reward or punishment? Does it seem cruel and arbitrary to us that we'd be separated from people we knew in our lives based on our actions?

Or is it simply the human condition that beckons us to take a scrying look into the great abyss of the unknown and divine some profound wisdom?

Humanity has struggled to understand and deal with death for as long as humans have been alive. All over the world, there are special funeral arrangements, services, and rituals that adherents to different religions follow to honor the departed's life and ensure that they find safe passage into the afterlife. The Greeks used to put coins on the eyes of a corpse as payment to the boatman Charon who would ferry the dead across the river Styx. The Hindus believe that cremation is the quickest way to release the soul of the dead to aid them in reincarnation.

This created a polarized worldview where on one end, those who believed in science completely denied the existence of an afterlife and refuted the existence of spirit, claiming that once you were dead, that was it. On the other end, you had adherents so afraid of going to hell that they bartered with clerics, trying to buy their way into heaven and avoiding hell by way of donation, confession, abstinence, and penance.

An over-reliance on any dogma can be considered extremist, even for those who look through the world with a scientific mindset. Science has yet to have all the answers, with many of its disciplines still in their infancy. To look to just science for answers is in itself a dogmatic practice known as scientism.

At the same time, abstaining from abstract activities deemed as sins just so you can avoid hell and get into heaven can, ironically, make a person miss out on living life. It also creates an opportunity for morally corrupt clergymen to abuse the faith of the vulnerable and the gullible. Televangelist pastors beckon you to curry God's favor by donating money to their megachurches.

And to think that all of that stems from a person's desire to fathom the afterlife.

Norse Paganism offers a comprehensive guide to the afterlife without being entirely factually didactic or by being admonishing. Unlike the Judeo-Christian worldview, one is not simply cursed to punishment in hell or rewarded eternally in heaven in Norse Paganism. A soul may travel to many different places if it wishes and may even choose to stay where it was buried. The Hel of Norse mythology was not like the Hell of Christianity. It was simply a place, not necessarily one of punishment.

But to understand the afterlife and the journey of the soul clearly, we must first understand how the Nordic people viewed the soul.

## The Self

The concept of a singular soul—such as the life force of a human being—is a Christian concept. According to the Norse worldview, the human self was a far more complex entity. You could say it was modular, with several different autonomous parts that could detach from one another, capable of existing independently. The Nordic concept of the self saw the body as an axiom upon which a person's spirit, perception, and will existed.

The self had four parts: The Hamr, the Hugr, the Fylgja, and the Hamingja.

## The Hamr

The Hamr meant the skin or shape of a person. The Hamr was the physical manifestation of one's self. It was the form that others could perceive in the real world. In other words, the Hamr was your outward body. In the Norse lore, your Hamr could change throughout your life, sometimes in evident ways such as through growing old from a kid into an adult and then into an aged person, and sometimes in abstract ways, such as how the color of a dead person changes from white to blue. The Hamr was not considered an absolute trait. It was alterable. Those who could shape-shift were gifted with the ability of Hamrhamr in which they could change their shape. One of the most prominent examples of this was Loki, who could alter his form at will.

**The Hugr**

This Hugr was an embodiment of your thoughts. Your personality, you're thinking, your manner of speaking, and all the quintessential things that made you unique in terms of character traits were all part of your Hugr. You may think of it as your consciousness. While the Hugr was considered an innate part of a person, it could cause changes far away. Those who possessed a strong Hugr could think about something and make it happen, much like having a strong sixth sense or possessing telekinesis.

**The Fylgja**

The Fylgja means follower. But what does that mean? Everyone has a Fylgja, an animal form related to a person's character. In European folklore, witches were symbolized as being surrounded by cats, owls, ravens, snakes, and toads—all of which were their familiar spirits, or Fylgja. The Fylgja can only be perceived by those who have a special sight. It is your familiar, whose well-being is tied to your well-being because if you die, your Fylgja will die as well, and if your Fylgja dies, you shall also die.

The Fylgja was also specific to the nature of a person. Someone who had a brave nature would have a lion as their Fylgja. A loyal person would have a dog or a horse as their Fylgja. A savage person could have a wolf as their familiar. Similarly, someone born in a noble house would have a bear as their Fylgja.

In life, if you feel drawn to a certain animal and feel as if there's some connection between you and them, or if some animal approaches you in a very magnetic way (a crow might caw at you and perch on your shoulder, a dog might wag its tail at you and lick your hands, a cat might purr and slide against your legs), there are chances that you possess the special sight that lets you see your familiar.

## The Hamingja

The Hamingja is the fourth part of the self, according to Norse lore. This part equates to your luck. Luck was seen as a quality that was inherent to a person and their familial lineage. It was considered just as much a trait of a person as their intelligence, strength, wisdom, or dexterity with a weapon. Luck was a tangible thing, a personal entity that both caused and expressed itself in a person's wealth, success, power, and fame.

When a person dies, their Hamingja is reincarnated in one of their descendants, especially if the child bears the name of their ancestor. The Hamingja could also be lent to others who direly needed it, such as someone suffering from poverty or a warrior going on an inquest.

The poem Hávamál attests to the modular belief in the self.

It says,

*"Wealth will pass,*

*Men will pass,*

*You too, likewise, will pass.*

*One thing alone Will never pass:*

*The fame of one who has earned it."*

It emphasizes that while your body may perish and your wealth will disappear, your legacy will live on, and through it, you shall live on. The belief that one's legacy and posthumous fame could practically ensure immortality through a life of hallowed remembrance was one of the reasons the Viking raiders were so fearless.

With such a complex concept of one's self, it is important to understand that there were several beliefs tied to these parts. For example, the Norse people believed in reincarnation. They held the belief that the Hugr of a person could transfer to the body of a newborn and that the Hamingja was something that kept passing down to your family at large.

A person, along with the components of their selves, could go to one of several places in the afterlife. Except for some cases (such as the death of brave warriors), the gods and goddesses did not pass judgment regarding reward or punishment for the departed.

### The Realms of the Afterlife

It was customary to give a funeral filled with traditions to the departed. Upon their death, a person's corpse was bestowed with specific personal belongings that represented what kind of person they were and what sort of profession they practiced in their lives.

For example, a nobleman was buried with gold and jewels. A craftsman was buried with the tools of his craft. A warrior was buried with their weapons. Whatever items were placed beside a dead person were believed to aid them in their afterlife.

Another tradition was sailing the dead away on top of a burning ship, which was believed to provide them with a safe passage into the next realm. If someone was buried underground, burial mounds made of stone were placed in such a way that they resembled the shape of a ship.

Regardless of the type of burial, some mandatory rituals had to be performed at every funeral. It was mandatory to dress up the dead in new clothes so that they'd have beautiful clothes to wear in the afterlife. The deceased's life was celebrated through drinking, eating, chanting, and singing.

The five places in the afterlife that the dead could go to include:

- Valhalla
- Fólkvangr
- Hel
- The Realm of Rán
- The Burial Mound

But this list only refers to the main afterlife realms. The scope of the Norse afterlife is not just limited to these alone. There are other realms, such as Gimle and Vingólf, where the dead can go. In some cases, the dead can reincarnate as their descendants or even reincarnate as elves. If someone lived a life of evil, they could even reincarnate in their corpse as a draugr.

## Valhalla

Also known as the Hall of the Fallen, this splendid place had a roof made of golden shields with spears for rafters. The seats surrounding the tables laden with food and drink were made of breastplates. Wolves guarded Valhalla. Eagles were said to fly above it. The dead who came here came to be known as einherjar. For someone to make it to Valhalla, they had to live a life of a brave warrior and then die a fitting death.

There were plentiful things to do in Valhalla besides just drinking and dining. The warriors would fight with each other, perform valiant acts, and take part in competitions. Each evening, their bodies would be restored to optimal health.

Ravenous from their daily effort, they'd take to the dining halls where they'd feed on the meat from the boar Sæhrímnir. This boar reincarnated itself every day after being slaughtered and butchered the day before, thus providing unending meat for the einherjar. The mead came from the udder of Heiðrún, a goat that provided endless supplies of mead. The einherjar dined with the Valkyries serving as their waitresses.

But lore tells us that this abode was not perceived as eternal. Upon the arrival of Ragnarök, Odin, the Valkyries, and the einherjar would leave Valhalla and take part in the final battle.

## Fólkvangr

The goddess Freya got the first pick from the crop of dead fallen warriors, taking them to a land that reflected her personality in terms of being kind, beautiful, peaceful, and elegant. Here, they could rest in the meadow and enjoy their time in the hall known as Sessrumnir, where Freya herself dwelled. This hall was described as beautiful, fair, and containing many seats to accommodate the dead.

According to some accounts, this place was not just reserved for warriors. One particular woman swore never to eat anything until she had a chance to dine with Freya. When she died of starvation, she was taken to Fólkvangr and rewarded for her belief in the goddess. Here, she got to dine with Freya again.

## Hel

The majority of people who die of old age or natural causes such as diseases go to Hel, which, unlike the Christian hell, is not a place of punishment but a place of existence where the dead rest. However, one particular place within Hel was reserved for the vilest of people, a place known as Nastrond, where Níðhöggr dwells. He fed on the bodies of these people as punishment for their inhumane actions.

## The Realm of Rán

Those who died at sea were said to go to the realm of Rán, a giantess who married Aegir, the lord of the sea. In Rán's realm, there were treasures that she had taken from the sailors that had died at sea. Both the sailors and their treasures rested in this realm with Rán.

## The Burial Mound

Sometimes, by choice, the dead could remain where they were buried and morph into a ghostly form known as haugbui. The haugbui was not considered a harmful entity like the draugr unless someone went out of their way to stomp on their burial mound. One can wonder why the haugbui chose to stay where they were buried. It was said that these people were so attached to the place where they had spent their lives that they were perfectly content staying here after passing, even in the form of ghosts.

However, if a person had been a terrible human being in their life, they did not get the chance to become a haugbui. Instead, they turned into a draugr, a malevolent being that could cause harm to others.

### Gimle

Have you wondered where the righteous souls who will fall in Ragnarök will go? There's a special place for them known as Gimle, a hall brighter than the sun, where there's eternal happiness for its residents.

### Vingólf

This enigmatic afterlife realm has quite contradictory origins. In some places, it is described as a hall where the gods and goddesses have assembled at times to drink ale and wine. In another mention, it was said to be a place just like Valhalla, where Odin sent the spirits of the brave fallen warriors. In a third instance, the name Vingólf is used interchangeably with Gimle. Regardless of its origins, this much is clear: It is an abode for those who were slain in battle.

From the account of the realms, we can gather that for everyone, whether they die of old age, drowning at sea, or falling in battle, there's a place in the next life. Those who wish to stay where they were in life can stay around their burial mounds as haugbui, content with where they are. As opposed to the afterlives of other religions, there's more agency provided in the afterlife belief of Norse mythology, a belief that does not entirely have to root itself in the concept of reward and punishment.

But there's also a stern reminder that in case of living a dishonorable life, a life filled with evil and malice and crime, there's punishment awaiting in the form of Nastrond or by distorting into a draugr, just as there's a warm promise for those who die bravely that there awaits a hall with a roaring fire, hot food, and cold mead.

However, those are the exceptions rather than the rule itself, meant to signify that while the gods are not particular in doling out unfair sentences upon the spirits of the dead, they're not disaffected or indifferent to the actions either. If someone has gone out of their way to live an immoral life filled with evil acts and has caused significant harm to others through murder and thievery, they're not going to get away with it. Similarly, if someone has been brave enough to earn Odin or Freya's favor, they will be redeemed in Valhalla or Fólkvangr.

### Pre-Christian Norse Afterlife

Some elements of Norse Paganism were influenced by the advent of Christianity, including the knowledge of a person's affair after death, making it extremely difficult to understand the original folklore about the afterlife. But through archaeological research, we know some things of the pre-Christian Norse beliefs about the afterlife, especially:

- You could be reunited with your ancestors and relatives after death, such as on the Holy Mountain known as Helgafjell, where people reunited with their friends, family, and ancestors after dying.
- You could spend your afterlife doing something that you enjoyed doing in your life.
- You could call upon your deceased ancestors to aid you in times of need, especially in times of strife. This was so because the line between death and life was blurry, and if the dead wished to intercede in affairs, they could reappear from the afterlife momentarily to help their living relatives.

# CHAPTER 8
## DIVINING RUNE WISDOM

Similar to how Aramaic, Arabic, and Sanskrit came to be formed as evolutionary tools of written communication by the world's Semitic, Arabic, and Indian populations, the runic alphabets were the first writing system to be used by the Germanic and Norse people.

But there was more to these runes than met the eye. Yes, they functioned on a primary level as letters with which words could be formed, but there was an ideographic and pictographic symbolism behind each rune. To use a rune in writing was more than just to note something down; it was to invoke the secret meaning and the hidden magical power of the rune itself. And that is the meaning of the word rune. It means "whisper," "secret," or "magic."

Every rune possessed a name that gave insight into its significance both in terms of its magical abilities and philosophical depiction of the visual appearance and the sound it made when you pronounced it. For instance, the Tiwaz rune was called the T-rune. It stood for Tiwaz, also known as Tyr. Tyr was thought to dwell in the sky, and thus, the T-rune was shaped like an arrow pointing up. This arrow also hints at Tyr's adroitness and prominence in warfare. Besides being used to form longer words, the T-rune was used solitarily as well as an ideograph as part of a magical spell that would grant victory in a battle.

The collective name for the runic alphabet is the futhark, named after the first six runes Fehu, Uruz, Thurisaz, Ansuz, Raidho, and Kaunan. There are three main futharks, namely the Elder Futhark, the Younger Futhark, and the Anglo-Saxon Futhorc.

# Elder Futhark

The Elder Futhark was the first to appear as a completely formed runic alphabets. Their development began in the first century CE and was said to be completed by the year 400. These had twenty-four characters, often divided into three families (Norse "ættir") of eight runes each, like so:

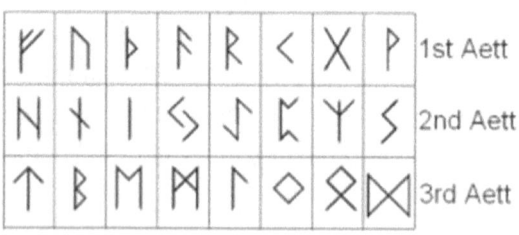

The Elder Futhark

# The Younger Futhark

A simplified version of the Elder Futhark, these were used during the Viking Age at around 750 CE and soon replaced the older alphabet in common use in Scandinavia. The Younger Futhark had sixteen characters.

# The Anglo-Saxon Futhorc

This thirty-three-character variant was adapted by the Anglo-Saxons to be used in England until the 9th and 10th centuries.

Runes were not commonly drawn on paper with pen and ink. Rather, they were etched onto wood, bone, metal, stone, and other hard surfaces. That's why they are so jagged, sharp, and angular.

Our present understanding of the futhark runes comes from the three rune poems documented in Iceland, England, and Norway, providing explanatory stanzas about each futhark.

## Where Did They Come From?

There are two accounts, one a chronological account tracked through history, detailing how the runes might have been derived from Italic alphabets, the other a mystical one telling the tale of Odin as he hung from Yggdrasil, pierced with a spear, and waiting for nine days until the meaning and shapes of the runes were revealed to him.

The first account tells us that the Mediterranean people who lived south of the Germanic population in the first century used Old Italic alphabets. With time, the Germanic tribes took to the Old Italic alphabet and derived their letters.

Tracing the runes through history tells us that the first runic inscription that archeologists found was on the Meldorf brooch in the north of Germany. It was dated back to 50 CE. The next appearance of runes is on the Vimose comb in Demark and the Øvre Stabu spearhead from Norway. Both these items date back to 150 CE. Keeping in chronological order, the earliest carving of the entire futhark appeared on the Kylver stone from Gotland, Sweden, dating back to 400 CE.

Now how did the runes in their primitive form travel from Germany to Northern Europe? The Germanic warbands were the most dominant military power of that time, and it is hypothesized that they carried the runes from one place to the other, taking inspiration from the Old Italic alphabets. During the Proto-Germanic period, Nordic people's ancestors worshiped Odin under his original name Woðanaz and associated runes with him.

For the Proto-Germanic people, Odin, or Woðanaz, was the epitome of divinity, wisdom, magic, and mystery. From their point of view, the runes did not come into existence from a source as drab as the Old Italic alphabet. They believed that the runes were not crafted or invented but were rather preternatural and preexisting, deciphered by Odin after he underwent a great sacrifice. According to the poem Hávamál, Odin hung himself from Yggdrasil, pierced by his spear, and sacrificed himself to himself, after which:

> "*No aid I received,*
>
> *Not even a sip from the horn.*
>
> *Peering down,*
>
> *I took up the runes –*
>
> *Screaming I grasped them –*
>
> *Then I fell back from there.*"

The runes seem to come from the waters of the Well of Urd, one of the wells that watered the Yggdrasil. This well was known to be a well of immense wisdom. This is corroborated by another poem called Völuspá:

> "*There stands an ash called Yggdrasil,*
>
> *A mighty tree showered in white hail.*
>
> *From there come the dews that fall in the valleys.*
>
> *It stands evergreen above Urd's Well.*
>
> *From there come maidens, very wise,*
>
> *Three from the lake that stands beneath the pole.*
>
> *One is called Urd, another Verdandi,*
>
> *Skuld the third; they carve into the tree*
>
> *The lives and fates of children.*"

The maidens mentioned in the poem are the Norns. The carvings in question are runes. From here, we can understand that the Well of Urd, the runes, magic, fate, and the Norns were all tied together.

As the lore continues, Odin presumably—after nine days of fasting and hanging—divined the runes by looking in the waters of the Well of Urd. Once he had understood the meaning and mysticism behind the runes, he imparted this wisdom to the humans, allowing rune masters to write down the significance of each rune and what it symbolized.

**What Do The Runes Symbolize?**

Plainly put, magic.

Cultures all over the world have attested to the existence of magic in some form or the other. Archaic languages, including Latin, Aramaic, Old Arabic, Sanskrit, and Persian, were all considered powerful enough for their words to serve as vessels of magic. In the pre-Christian Germanic worldview, the same belief was held. People believed in the power of words, believing that the correct pronunciation and the right utterance of a proper word could create an effect that would be difficult to describe in terms other than magical. The ancient Nordic people held the belief that words shaped reality. Words spoken and woven into sentences could create a powerful impact, sending forth energy into the world that could never be taken back.

The philosophy and symbolism of runes were intricately linked to the understanding that language structured one's perception. That thinking outside of language was virtually impossible because all thoughts took shape within the confines of one's language. In Proto-Germanic society, if one were to utter something out loud and make their thoughts public by way of speaking, it was considered to be made a part of the fabric of reality itself, going so far as to alter reality to make room for this new vocalization.

Coming back to runes, each rune represented a phoneme. A phoneme is the smallest unit of sound in linguistics. Letters such as a, b, s, t, and r are all considered phonemes. Each rune was considered the depiction of its phoneme in a visual form. Each phoneme also carries an innate meaning, which can be used collectively in the form of a word to give characteristics to the item or action being described by that word. This theory is known as phonosemantics, stating that there's an intricate connection between the sounds that comprise a word and the meaning of the word itself.

In simpler terms, there was a deep connection between the runes used to form a particular word, and this connection alluded to the mystery of the runes that Odin deciphered in the first place. Each of these connections was not an arbitrary connection but a meaningful one, extending not just to the relationship between the word and its phonemes but also to the word and its visual representation in the form of runes.

This sophisticated approach to language meant that runes weren't just a means for two people to communicate with each other but also a mode of communication between humans and the invisible powers and entities that surrounded them, such as magic, spirits, and gods.

The Eddas and sagas provide a testament to the fact that the runes possess magical attributes that work in a particular way. One example of that comes from Egil's Saga, in which Egil stops by a farmer's house to eat a meal. The farmer's daughter is severely ill. The farmer asks Egil for help. Egil investigates and discovers a whalebone with runes carved into it. Egil, a rune master, understands that the runes on the whalebone are causing the girl's illness. He scratches away the runes and burns the whalebone, then writes a different set of runes meant to counteract the effects of the previous runes. In time, the farmer's daughter recovers from her illness.

Even the Norns used runes to inscribe the fates of all living beings, suggesting that the runes were inherently magical.

Furthermore, the Rune Poems also attested to the existence of both phonological representation and inherent meaning of each rune.

**What Do The Runes Mean?**

Based on the meanings provided by the Rune Poems, here are the definitions of the twenty-four Elder Futhark runes.

**Name:** Fehu. **Phoneme:** F. **Represents:** Cattle. **Meaning:** Wealth, Success, Fertility, Abundance, Security.

The f-rune denotes money and material gain. It also symbolizes coming into wealth as well as accumulating wealth. A deeper meaning of this rune is destruction and sorrow if you choose to be stingy with your money and don't share it with those in dire need. It harkens you to follow a balanced path where you both spend your money and save it for future use. Another meaning of the f-rune is cattle, connoting the features of livestock such as sustenance and creation (Auðumbla being the primeval cow).

**Name:** Uruz. **Phoneme:** U. **Represents:** Bull. **Meaning:** Strength, Force, Wild, Freedom, Courage, Sagacity.

The u-rune symbolizes an extinct species of ox known as the aurochs. This animal used to inhabit Europe once upon a time and was considered an elemental force of nature. Much like the animal, the u-rune is a symbol of strength and equates to a human being's ability to defend themselves against danger and bring about positive change in their lives through courage.

**Name:** Thurisaz. **Phoneme:** Th. **Represents:** Thorn. **Meaning:** Danger, Conflict, Suffering, Sudden Reaction, Defense.

This rune is about brute strength, such as that wielded by Thor. You may use this strength to remove objects hindering your path or vanquish your foes. Another meaning of this rune is that of thorn, representing danger that lies hidden much like a thorn, only to pierce you suddenly. But this is a forewarning rather than a threat. You may prepare yourself for whatever challenges lay ahead by being stronger and more aware of your surroundings.

**Name:** Ansuz. **Phoneme:** A. **Represents:** Estuary or the Æsir god. **Meaning:** Communication, Talking, Mouth, Understanding, Inspiration, Prosperity.

This is a meta-rune, symbolizing the discovery of runes by Odin himself. As Odin once perceived the runes and conveyed their meaning to mortals, you too can communicate with others. This rune is also associated with Loki's intelligence, wisdom, and unusual insight. Combing both meanings, this rune equates to speech and the ability to convince others through your words.

**Name:** Raidho. **Phoneme:** R. **Represents:** Wagon or Horseback Journey. **Meaning:** Traveling, Journeying, Evolution, Rhythm, Movement, Growth.

The r-rune symbolizes a horseback journey or a wagon, signifying a journey. It may be a physical journey that takes you to different lands for better job opportunities or leisure or a spiritual journey that allows you to know more about yourself and the world around you. Raidho represents the evolution one undergoes after journeying from one place to another.

**Name:** Kaunan. **Phoneme:** K. **Represents:** Torch or Ulcer. **Meaning:** Pain, Mortality, Life.

With two apparent meanings, the k-rune is associated with ulcers/sores and fire/torch. As a symbol of an ulcer, this rune foreshadows pain and suffering. As a torch, it represents the enlightenment that one gets after lighting a controlled fire.

**Name:** Gebo. **Phoneme:** G. **Represents:** Gift. **Meaning:** Generosity, Exchange, Partnership, Relationship, Friendliness.

The g-rune is all about gift-giving and appreciating someone who gives you gifts. Giving someone gifts was considered a noble act in Norse culture, and it was a reciprocated act, meaning if someone gave you a gift, you had to give them one as well, which resulted in strengthening friendships and relationships. Gebo is also symbolic of the sexual union between two people through the act of gift-giving.

**Name:** Wunjo. **Phoneme:** W. **Represents:** Joy. **Meaning:** Pleasure, Prosperity, Happiness, Success, Comfort.

The w-rune means pleasure, upcoming happiness, and prosperous living. If you see this rune during meditation or divination, know that it's a good omen, telling you to be grateful for what you have and to be appreciative of what you will achieve soon.

**Name:** Hagalaz. **Phoneme:** H. **Represents:** Hail. **Meaning:** Nature, Challenges, Anger, Adversity.

The h-rune symbolizes hail, a destructive force of nature, foretelling the advent of calamity. Rather than cower from misfortune, one must seek to rise to the challenge and evolve into a better person as a result of adversity.

**Name:** Naudhiz. **Phoneme:** N. **Represents:** Need. **Meaning:** Conflict, Endurance, Independence, Self-Actualization, Willpower.

The n-rune represents need. It also represents the necessity of pain in this life. As the h-rune symbolizes adversity, the n-rune leads you to the realization that sometimes adversity and pain are necessary catalysts for personal growth.

**Name:** Isaza. **Phoneme:** I. **Represents:** Ice. **Meaning:** Clarity, Introspection, Waiting, Challenges.

The i-rune is symbolic of ice. It equates to two particular things. First, the clarity of clear ice, such as on the surface of a lake in the winter, alludes to one becoming wiser and seeing things as they are. The second meaning of this rune refers to the barren nature of winter where frost hinders the growth of crops and subdues even the strongest of people into the confines of their homes.

**Name:** Jera. **Phoneme:** J. **Represents:** Year. **Meaning:** Cyclical Nature, Completion of Things, Changes in Things, Harvesting Time.

The j-rune stands for a year, especially a year that had a good harvest. This rune signifies the cyclical nature of time. For people who have spent a long time trying to accomplish something, this rune can bring the good news of expecting a great result.

**Name:** Eihwaz. **Phoneme:** I. **Represents:** Yew Tree. **Meaning:** The World Tree, Enlightenment, Knowledge, Finding Balance, Death.

The i-rune stands for the yew tree, and as such, it represents the wisdom of Yggdrasil, the strength that is associated with trees, and finding balance in life. A yew tree, with its branches extending into the sky and its roots running deep into the ground, is the epitome of stability and balance.

**Name:** Perthro. **Phoneme:** P. **Represents:** Dice Cup. **Meaning:** Chance, Fate, Destiny, Luck.

The p-rune symbolizes the dice cup, and it can mean anything from taking chances, putting your faith in your luck, and accepting your destiny. Casting a dice cup and letting the dice fall as they may is innately a very fate-affirming activity where you make peace with the fact that whatever number the dice show is tied to your luck.

**Name:** Algiz. **Phoneme:** Z. **Represents:** Elk. **Meaning:** Guarding Something, Protection, Defensiveness.

The z-rune represents the majestic elk. Just as elks represent grandeur, strength, and power, this rune represents protection, defensiveness, and the strength required to guard those close to you.

**Name:** Sowilo. **Phoneme:** S. **Represents:** Sun. **Meaning:** Nurturing, Cleansing, Health, Resources.

The s-rune denotes the sun and symbolizes the nurturing elements of sunlight, such as providing energy, bringing warm light, and making the crops grow. The sun is an infinite resource; its light is considered one of the most vital necessities for all life on this planet. It encompasses the entire biosphere. In this regard, the s-rune is considered a benevolent rune.

**Name:** Tiwaz. **Phoneme:** T. **Represents:** Tyr. **Meaning:** Justice, Logic, Masculinity, Self-Sacrifice,

Self-Discipline. The t-rune is associated with the brave god Tyr, who, above all, chose self-sacrifice when he placed his hand inside Fenrir's mouth to subdue the wolf. Tyr was wise, logical, and quite strong. He was also a champion of justice. All of those traits are embodied in this rune.

**Name:** Berkanan. **Phoneme:** B. **Represents:** Birch Tree. **Meaning:** Femininity, Healing, Birth, Fertility.

The b-rune stands for the birch tree, a symbol of fertility, growth, and nurturing. This rune is associated with Nerthus, a goddess of fertility. This rune is said to preside over the four domains of life—birth, coming of age, marriage, and death.

**Name:** Ehwaz. **Phoneme:** E. **Represents:** Horse. **Meaning:** Journey, Transportation, Movement, Progress.

The e-rune attests to the relationship between a man and his horse. This bond was a strong one, tethered with loyalty, cooperation, and teamwork. A horse was symbolic of journeying, progressing through life, and being man's steadfast companion through thick and thin. In that regard, the e-rune is a benevolent rune.

**Name:** Mannaz. **Phoneme:** M. **Represents:** Humanity. **Meaning:** Cooperativeness, Society, Helping, Individuality.

The m-rune represents humanity in general and what sets humanity apart from other creatures. It symbolizes intelligence, wisdom, the ability to communicate, individuality, personality, societal relations, and culture.

**Name:** Laguz. **Phoneme:** L. **Represents:** Water. **Meaning:** Formlessness, Flow, Potentiality, Emotions, Depth, Hopes, Fears, Dreams, Rejuvenation.

The l-rune symbolizes water bodies such as lakes and seas. In its formlessness, water is filled with potentiality. It can be used to nourish fields and quench one's thirst, but just as easily, it can be an agent of chaos in the form of torrential rain and floods. But here, within the context of this rune, the nature of water is seen as beneficial. Water is the source of life and growth. The l-rune also implies fluidity of thoughts, emotions, and the depth of one's subconscious mind, where dreams, hopes, and fears dwell.

**Name:** Ingwaz. **Phoneme:** Ng. **Represents:** Seed. **Meaning:** Growth, Wisdom, Change, New Beginnings.

Ingwaz is associated with Frey. This rune signifies male fertility, peace, resting, attunement to nature, wisdom, and the evolution of one's psyche. This rune is also symbolic of completion, whether of a journey or a project.

**Name:** Dagaz. **Phoneme:** D. **Represents:** Dawn. **Meaning:** Awakening, Illumination, Completion, Hope, Certainty.

The d-rune represents the day. With daylight comes a new beginning. People deep in their slumbers wake up and head out to meet the day. With daylight, the shadow of the night passes, allowing illumination to light up all the fields, mountains, forests, rivers, and seas. To the travelers stuck in the dark, daylight comes bearing hope, telling them it is safe to travel again. Unlike the uncertainty that comes with the darkness of the night, this benign daylight establishes certainty.

**Name:** Othalan. **Phoneme:** O. **Represents:** Inheritance. **Meaning:** Heritage, Possessions, Experience, Value, Ancestry.

The o-rune represents your heritage and inheritance. This can be taken in a tangible meaning, such as the estate your ancestors left you or it can be understood metaphorically, such as your genetics and the tradition you carry on. You can also use this as the monogram for Odin.

## Modern Rune Usage

Followers of Norse Paganism use runes in their practices in three main ways:

### Carving

The intent behind carving particular runes on rock, stone, bone, or any other surface is to open a channel of communication between the carver and the invisible world of gods, magic, and fate. In terms of invocation, rune-carving is the easiest and simplest form of veneration, invoking and hallowing a deity. One must understand that the runes have both an intrinsic and extrinsic representation, the latter being that of the cosmos, gods, fate, and magic, while the former being the representation of the human subconscious or psyche.

Traditionally, practitioners would carve the rune's outline into a surface, then coat it with blood, red dye, or crimson paint.

It should be noted that runic carving did not originate from a single source, so its usage had and continues to have variations from practitioner to practitioner.

The inherent intention, however, is the same. When carved onto a surface, the runes serve as a device that allows you to communicate with the primeval forces of nature, with the spirits of your ancestors, and most importantly, with the gods and goddesses whose favor you are trying to seek.

**Divination**

Divination using runes allows you to tap into your intuition, communicate with forces greater than you, and understand the significance of certain events. You may even foretell something that'll happen in the future.

Of the several types of runic divination, the simplest form is using a single rune for yes or no answers. The runemaster should ask a question, then proceed to take out a rune from the bag. Based on its symbol and meaning and the intuitive feeling the runemaster gets, the answer may incline towards a yes or a no.

Then there's the three-rune casting method, in which the runes were cast in multiples of three, representing the past, present, and future or situation, action, and outcome.

The most traditional way of runic divination is to cast or throw runes on a piece of white fabric while looking to the heavens and then reading only the runes that landed in the upright position.

Additionally, more experienced runemasters can use different layouts, such as the five-rune layout, the seven-rune layout, and the twenty-four-rune layout.

In the five-rune layout, the runes are laid out in the form of a cross with a question in mind. The runes at the bottom connote the basic elements that influence the question. The runes on the left highlight the problems surrounding the question. The runes on the top show the positives about the question. The runes on the right show the immediate answer to the question. Lastly, the rune in the middle shows the impact of the future on the question.

### Meditation/Hallowing

Runes have inherent magical qualities that you can use to meditate. But because this is an open-ended practice with numerous interpretations and manifestations, this form of rune usage is considered very elusive and difficult. The principle behind meditation and hallowing using runes is to use carved/drawn runes for contemplation. One can contemplate the runes consciously in an attempt to uncover their mysticism so that one can better understand the universe and the events that take place within it, especially events that are going to take place in the future. One may even meditate upon the runes to tap into their powers.

For any three of these practices, you can build a dedicated altar where you can decorate the space with runes, symbols related to the runes, and whatever offerings you want to present to the gods. Additionally, you can carve your own runes or buy pre-carved ones from a store that sells paganism and heathenry supplies.

Runic magic takes quite some time to learn. Disciplines like runic divination and meditation require a lot of patience and effort before they can bear fruit. If you are just getting into runes, my advice to you would be to keep at it. The answers you seek are just within your reach. Remember Odin and how he suffered for nine days, hanging upside down from the tree. It was only after he had gone through a great ordeal that the runes became known to him.

Once the mystery of the runes manifests itself to you, you will thank yourself for sticking with this elusive, arcane, and powerful discipline. The mysticism behind the runes is not static. It's a dynamic discipline, with the meaning of the runes changing with context, deepening with wisdom, and becoming clearer with age.

# CHAPTER 9
# RITES OF PASSAGE

The Norse people had managed to not only survive but thrive in the face of harsh environmental challenges. As a people, they braved frosty winters and defended their towns from attacks by wild animals and rival warring tribes alike. They suffered through the severest spells of harsh weather when food and water were scarce, and primitive medicine was all they had to treat illnesses. They did not have access to advanced medicine such as vaccination nor had created intricate surgical procedures to save the lives of injured people or patients suffering from terminal diseases.

As a result, the mortality rate was quite high, not just in children but in adults as well. Upon the birth of a child, their life expectancy was merely twenty-years-old. Half of the infants who survived their births would just live till seven years. Half the population of their communities was made up of children less than the age of fifteen. Of the people who reached the age of twenty, only half would live to see the age of fifty. A mere one to three percent of the population has ever reached over the age of sixty. All of this was attributed to the high rate of mortality.

In those times, the birth process was precarious for both the mother and the child. The mother was susceptible, and there was a good chance that she could die during childbirth. As a result of the high infant mortality rate, it was not uncommon for Norse women to give birth to up to seven children in their lifetime. This mortality rate meant that most parents did not grow old enough to watch their children marry. Fewer grew old enough to see their grandchildren.

What do you think comes out of this much suffering? When at long last the Nordic people got a break, what was their reaction? They would celebrate wholeheartedly, reveling in their many ways by drinking, dancing, feasting, and venerating the gods. The harsher their conditions, the fiercer they celebrated whenever they appeared victorious, giving birth to many rites of passage and rituals that signify the importance of events such as childbirth and marriage.

**Marriage**

Norse weddings marked an occasion of celebration where two families came together as one. Marriage represented more than just the unification of man and woman. Norse people, particularly Vikings, built their families around the concept of alliances. In this way, a marriage between a man and woman was just as much an alliance of both families.

Before two people could marry each other, many negotiatory talks took place between both families. People from both sides of the family would come together and discuss different terms and conditions, including the price paid for the bride. This was known as mundr.

During these talks, they would also discuss peace treaties between the families and their allies and put forth terms to share their riches and wealth, such as their inheritances.

Norse weddings always took place on Frigg's day, given that Frigg was considered the goddess of love, familiar harmony, fertility, and childbirth, thus being the embodiment of a rite as fundamental as a wedding.

As this was an event that called for much preparation in the form of ceremony, drinking, and feasting, the people had to choose the most opportune date based on what the weather would be like on that day. This was to ensure that the ceremony could take place outdoors. Many guests would arrive from out of town, and preparations would have to be made for their lodging.

It was a mandatory—one could even say legal—requirement for the groom and bride to drink the honeyed mead during their wedding and for the remainder of the first month of their marriage, which lasted a moon cycle. And yes, this is where the concept of honeymoon comes from. One apparent reason for this obligatory month-long drinking rite was to facilitate conception. The other, less apparent, was to make the newlyweds comfortable with each other, letting relaxation and uninhibited time take hold of them so they could become better acquainted with each other in every sense of the word. We'll get to the why of it in a second.

Wedding celebrations were a matter of extreme mirth to both families and their extended relatives as well as their friends. The celebrations were spread over an entire week. The week-long length of the celebrations made the timing very critical, as it had to be arranged during a time when the harvest was readily available, and it wasn't snowing outdoors.

The bride and groom had special activities to perform preceding the wedding. First, the woman had to find a gift to give her husband on the morning after their first night together. Next, the bride would go to a bathhouse with the married members of her family. There, the women would remove a kransen (a circlet that symbolizes virginity) and place it in a box for the bride to give to her future daughter. The bride-to-be would then cleanse herself with steaming water, switch herself with twigs, and jump into cool water to completely clean her body.

While all this transpired on the women's front, the men took the groom for graverobbing. Yes, they would take the groom to the grave of his ancestor, from where he would have to take out a sword. This represented the man coming into his own and stepping into a new life.

Dirty from graverobbing, the groom would also head to the bathhouse and clean himself thoroughly.

Once they'd both cleaned themselves, they would dress festively for their ceremony. Nordic traditions paid more importance to hair than they did to dresses, as a woman's hair was a symbol of her femininity and sexuality. The longer and more decorative her hair, the more feminine and sexual she was considered. The bride was also adorned with a bridal crown that was passed down from mother to daughter through the ages. The groom would also oil and wax his hair, mustache, and beard. He would also wear the symbol of Thor, the hammer, as it was considered vital to fertility. Thor had a considerable role in the wedding ceremony. The bride would invoke Thor to bless her and the ceremony. Then she'd place a hammer upon her lap to ask for stronger children.

The legalities of the wedding—such as the exchange of goods, discussion of the estate, and finalization of mundr —took place before the main ceremony.

The main ceremony would also contain religious rituals such as blood sacrifice. The person who arranged the wedding, also known as the Gothi, would sacrifice a cow to Freya to bless the marriage.

The bride and groom would exchange swords and rings. The groom would give her the sword he got from his ancestor's grave, while the bride would give him a sword that was passed down to her family. Her giving him the sword would symbolize the passing of the role of her protection from her father to her husband. Through the exchange of swords, the two families became connected. From this moment onwards, both families would be responsible for each other, including protecting each other and interceding on each other's behalf.

While the swords interlinked the families together, the rings joined the groom and bride with each other.

Then there would be a foot race between the two families. Whichever family reached the feast hall first would win and get beer and mead served to them for the rest of the ceremony by the losing family. It was customary to let the bride and her family win the race so that the groom would approach her and carry her into his arms into the hall.

After a copious amount of drinking on the part of the bride, groom, and guests, they would feast on delicious dishes.

Since more often than not Norse marriages were arranged, meaning the two didn't know a lot about each other before, the honeymoon concept came about. The bride and groom were expected to acquaint themselves with each other during this time.

## Childbirth and the Naming Ceremony

The arrival of a newborn was a highly anticipated event in Nordic culture. People would gather around the expecting wife and sing songs imbued with magic and invocation to the goddesses to ensure that the woman would give birth properly and the child would come into the world healthy.

The Norse women gave birth in their homes. This was an absolute necessity, both culturally and also because the women preferred to give birth in the comfort of their homes. Once a woman was eight months pregnant, she never left the confines of her home. Her husband also stayed with her. He was obligated to stay in the house with the expecting mother, regardless of his designation. He'd delegate someone else to perform his job and duties. When his child was born, the father has to perform a ceremony that would dub the child a person. He also had to be present during the birth, in the same room. This was legally enforced.

After the mother gave birth to the child (which, unlike modern methods of birth, was done upright), both of them were cleaned thoroughly. The child was wiped clean, and it was made sure that they were breathing properly. Then the mother accepted her child as hers by nursing it for the first time. During the first nursing, other witnesses, such as the midwife and the husband, had to be present.

During the first nine days, the child and the mother were taken care of, and more witnesses gathered for the upcoming ritual. During this time, the name was also finalized between relatives.

After nine days, the father took the baby and placed them on his knee. There, he saw the child and acknowledged that this was indeed his child. Then he sprinkled the baby with water and proceeded to name them.

The naming was not an arbitrary ritual. Norse people paid special significance to names, believing that names could give the child a certain trait. The names could also invoke the blessing of a god. They were also used as ancestor worship, as many Norse people named their children after their ancestors. Once chosen and given, the name was known to carry religious, spiritual, mystical, and ancestral significance.

Once the baby was named, they were considered a complete person, a fully-formed human being. After this, the mother went back to her daily duties in a matter of three days. If she were sick, she'd take a bit longer to recover, and then return to her regular routine.

Some accounts suggest that mothers fed their babies for up to two to four years, depending upon the availability of food and climate conditions. If other provisions were plentiful, she would wean the child earlier than four years, believing that the earlier the child was weaned and given proper food, the better their chances of survival. As a rule of thumb, most children were weaned at the age of two years. Regardless of how long the mother nursed the child, she kept the child by her side for one year after their birth, meaning she would literally strap the child to her side and carry it around everywhere she went.

Once the child was old enough to sleep on their own, they'd get a crib or a cradle.

When a child grew up, they would follow in their parent's footsteps. Let's say someone's father was a swordsmith; then the child would learn the principles of the craft from their father and assist them at the forge with their daily chores.

Children were expected to help around the house, including herding cattle, working the crops, and gathering firewood and fruits from the forest.

But life was not all work and chores for the kids. They were allowed to socialize with other kids their age and even play with toys. The boys were given wooden swords, shields, and smaller bows at an early age to learn the art of battle. Their elder brothers or father would teach them how to swing swords, raise their shields, and perfect their bow aim.

# CHAPTER 10
## PRACTICING MODERN PAGANISM

You can declare yourself a pagan by affirming the existence of the Norse gods and goddesses and making them an integral part of your life. If you already believe in them, feel their presence, and are influenced by their traits, then you are well on your way to becoming a practicing pagan.

While the old Norse religion does not exist in its original form, several branches of Neo-Paganism have emerged over the years, such as Asatru, Vanatru, Rökkatru, Heathenry, Odinism, and Thursatru, all of which serve to venerate the Norse gods and goddesses and recreate the old Norse religion that was followed more than a thousand years ago.

You may choose which form of Norse Paganism you most resonate with. There are as many forms today that are just as diverse in their practices and beliefs as the old Norse religion was. If you are more of an introvert and prefer worship and meditation in solitude, there are options for you, and if you're an extrovert who gets a kick out of community-based rituals and worship, there are avenues for you as well. While some branches have chosen to remain as authentic as possible, sticking closely to the original Norse religion in terms of practices, others have taken a dynamic turn and have adapted with the times, embodying the beliefs in evolved practices that are suitable to the modern era.

If the diminishing of the original old Norse religion upon the advent of Christianity can be likened to Ragnarök, then the resurgence of modern neo-paganism in the form of various branches of paganism and heathenry can be considered a rebirth of the world. A world that's getting populated by more and more pagans every day. Asatru, one of the forms of paganism practiced today, is now considered to be the fastest-growing religion in Iceland. Since 2007, the religion has seen a growth of more than 200%

Before you formally begin your journey into paganism, some things are expected from you:

- Growth. You will undergo both spiritual and mental growth as a result of walking along the pagan path.
- Individuality. As you walk further along this path, you will become your own person and will break free from conformity.
- Devotion. The best way to become a pagan is to do your fair share of research by reading the relevant literature and understanding the philosophies and mysticism of Norse Mythology. This is a feat that requires devotion.

Paganism does not demand you to be some prophesied chosen one who has registered with Mensa. Paganism accepts you as you are. You don't have to be special to venerate the gods and bring them into your life. You are completely fine as you are. In fact, this is one of the principles of paganism in general; accepting yourself for who you are and making peace with it. Embodying the principles of paganism in your daily life will allow you to live a more grateful, enjoyable, fulfilling, and wholesome life. So, without further ado, let's look at the different forms of Norse Paganism available today. Know that there's no wrong answer, and then go from there.

**Asatru**

Asatru is a neo-pagan revivalist religion that seeks to venerate the Æsir gods. Asatru's main focus is the gods Odin, Thor, Frigg, Tyr, Baldur, and other Æsir deities. The revival of Asatru took place relatively recently in 1973.

It came into existence after Sveinbjörn Beinteinsson, who was originally a farmer but later became the first high priest of his organization. He petitioned the Icelandic government, asking them to acknowledge the Icelandic Asatru Fellowship as a real religion. His appeal became successful and later on the religion was even acknowledged in Denmark and Norway. Today, there are more than twenty-thousand followers of Asatru all over the world.

Asatru's teachings come from the Eddas written by Snorri Sturluson. While there is no one set scripture, the adherents of Asatru do follow a collected medieval Icelandic book known as the Codex Regis which is based on Snorri's writings.

The priests in Asatru are known as Goði. They are responsible for performing ceremonies such as marriages, funerals, and blót.

The essence of Asatru is peace and tolerance. To that effect, Asatru disowns militarism and the glorification of battle, bloodshed, and military heroism.

**Vanatru**

Just as Asatru serves to venerate the Æsir gods, Vanatru is the denomination of Paganism wherein worship and veneration are focused on the Vanir such as Njord, Freya, and Frey.

While there are followers of Vanatru out there, Vanatru does not have a particular creed, a sacred book, rituals, or details about how Vanatru was created and who was behind it. Among this obscurity, there are a few depictions of Frey and Freya, as well as a couple of stories from the Eddas in which the three Vanir are mentioned.

This much is clear, though: this was a religion followed by people in the past, but as Christianity came to Scandinavia, it seemed to vanish.

Yet, the adherents to Vanatru still devotedly worship Freya and Frey and Njord, believing that the Vanir are still just as alive today as they were more than a thousand years ago, and so, even without a lot to go on, people have managed to reconnect with the Vanir gods and have created a beautiful religion centered around the Vanir.

This ambiguity has allowed followers of Vanatru to intuitively connect with the gods through meditation, divination, veneration, and runes.

Vanatru sets itself apart from Asatru by focusing on folk magic, divination, witchcraft, and rituals that serve to communicate directly with the Vanir gods and goddesses.

## Rökkatru

It is completely natural if you don't feel as drawn to the Æsir and Vanir as you thought. Maybe, you are more in tune with the Rökkr, and perhaps the Rökkr beckon you toward them. While the Asatru and Vanatru followers venerate the Æsir and Vanir, respectively, the followers of Rökkatru venerate Loki, Hel, Fenrir, Jörmungandr, and Angrboða.

In short, the agents of Ragnarök. The name Rökkr itself refers to Ragnarök. Rökkatru also venerates the Jötnar.

This denomination seeks to liberate its followers from the polarity of good and evil, black and white. The Rökkr are not enemies and are not considered evil by those who follow Rökkatru. They are as fundamental to the existence of the Nine Realms as the Æsir and Vanir. The Rökkatru followers hold the belief that the actions of the Rökkr are a dire necessity so that the universe can be born anew again. Otherwise, without Ragnarök, what would be the point?

Followers of Rökkatru perform heathen magical practices such as seiðr. They also venerate the deities using altars, communicate with them through meditation, and even perform astral projection methods, including path walking and journeying. Rökkatru rituals also utilize runes and invocations.

## Thursatru

Rökkatru and Thursatru resemble the left-hand path in terms of embracing the darker aspect of Norse mythology. Thursatru, similarly, embraces the chaotic nature of Norse myth, not shying away from it. Rather, it venerates the anti-cosmic forces known as Thurses (Jötunns), including beings such as Ymir, Loki, Hel, Jörmungandr, Níðhöggr, and Gullveig—all of which are beings that resonate with chaos.

If you want to put it into terms of traditional religions, Thursatru is the Satanism to Asatru and Vanatru's Christianity. It embraces the anti-Æsir, and the anti-Vanir, and looks forward to the coming of Ragnarök, not within an evil capacity but in an anticipatory capacity.

The rebellious nature of Thursatru has allowed its followers to be very individualistic in terms of their practices.

Whereas Asatru, Odinism, and other forms of Heathenry employ the Nine Noble Virtues in their belief system, the Thursatru followers do not adhere to these principles.

**The Nine Noble Virtues include:**

1. Courage
2. Truth
3. Honor
4. Fidelity
5. Discipline
6. Hospitality
7. Self-Reliance
8. Industriousness
9. Perseverance

While heathens and pagans use these virtues as a guide in their daily lives, those who adhere to Rökkatru and Thursatru tend to live life on their own terms, dismissing the notion of the virtues.

In regards to worship, Thursatru followers make offerings to the Jötunn, build altars, venerate, meditate, and even perform rune magic meant to appease the Jötunn.

If all the main branches of paganism are like different genres of heavy metal, Thursatru revels in considering itself the death metal of paganism.

## Odinism

Odinism contains many of the same beliefs as Asatru, and both denominations are quite similar to each other. At one point, in 1997, Odinism and Asatru joined as one, but later on, because of a reason, the union was dissolved in 2002.

Some far-right, racist groups decided to make Odinism their banner for white supremacy, which gave Odinism a bad name, going so far as to make other branches of heathenry and paganism disassociate with it completely. This is not true of all branches but it is important to be aware of.

But racism and white supremacy is not what Odinism is about. In its purest form, Odinism venerates Odin and his Æsir kin. The majority of the beliefs come from the Eddas and poems, with an emphasis on Odin and his character.

Odinism has its own values quite similar to the nine noble virtues, all of which are inspired by Odin's tales and his characteristics. They are:

1. Strength is better than weakness
2. Courage is better than cowardice
3. Joy is better than guilt
4. Honor is better than dishonor
5. Freedom is better than slavery
6. Kinship is better than alienation
7. Realism is better than dogmatism
8. Vigor is better than lifelessness
9. Ancestry is better than rootlessness.

The mode of worship and veneration in Odinism resembles Asatru and Vanatru, as the basic idea behind veneration is the remembrance of gods, honoring their lives, and attempting to become like them. Odinists also observe the blóts that followers of Asatru observe.

By definition, such as seen in the Odinistic values, Odinism is a proactive religion. The Odin brotherhood goes so far as to distinguish itself, stating that while others hug trees, we cut them down and build fires from them. While others hold hands, we make fists. While others pet animals, we hunt them as prey.

Unfortunately, the fixation of the white nationalist and far-right movements on Odinism as a symbol of white supremacy has marred the name of an otherwise pure and sincere branch of Paganism.

**Lokeans**

Lokeans, much like those who follow Rökkatru, observe that Loki is not a force of evil or a devilish figure but an instigator of change, a patron of those who think outside of the box and don't fit into societal structures and traditional norms, and can transcend into a higher form using his shapeshifting powers.

Lokeans worship and venerate Loki as their primary deity, making offerings to him, seeking his counsel, and performing rituals that attract his attention.

Lokeans believe in finding Loki's energy and incorporating it into their daily lives.

They pray to him and share their thoughts with him, sometimes in a one-sided conversation, but other times, they get insight and whispers from Loki.

They make offerings such as mead and ale to him and even hold a Blót for him in a formal sense. Lokeans also set up a shrine in honor of Loki and worship him at an altar.

Lokeans stand by the principle that Norse mythology does not have distinct good and evil. They believe that Loki, while, yes, sometimes caused chaos, that chaos was necessary and meaningful.

Lokeans are still polytheistic, acknowledging the existence and importance of other deities within the Norse pantheon.

Other aspects that attract Lokeans to Loki include his sexual and gender fluidity, the extreme lengths he goes to achieve his goals (remember when he got Balder killed?), and how he is the harbinger of change. Loki faced change with a brave face and embraced it rather than cowering from it. Lokeans try to embody this principle.

**Heathenry**

Those who adhere to heathenry state that our ancestors were collectively heathens before the Christianization of the world. This statement does not limit itself to Scandinavia. In pre-Islamic Arabia, there was an entire pantheon of Arabic deities, such as Laat, Uzza, and Manat, that the Arabs used to worship and venerate before the arrival of Islam. In South Asia, the predominant population was Hindu and worshipped hundreds of thousands of different deities before missionaries from Europe and Arabia came and converted many of the people to Islam and Christianity.

Heathenry takes this belief and offers its followers to go back to the religion of their ancestors. The diverse belief system of heathenry encompasses beliefs from the old Norse religion, with influences from other heathen practices from other parts of the world as well, creating further denominations such as Frankish Heathenry, Gothic Heathenry, Saxon Heathenry, Frisian Heathenry, and Anglo-Saxon Heathenry.

Modern Heathenry takes the fundamental beliefs of Frith, Honor, Luck, Gifting Cycle, and Wyrd and Orlæg as its foundation.

**Frith** —A sense of peace, security, and inviolability that comes from making covenants not to harm each other.

**Honor** — Honor in ancient Germanic represented a person's usefulness to the community. An honorable person benefited their society, while someone with no honor caused the community a lot of harm.

**Luck** — Similar to the fate described in Norse Paganism, the heathen variant of luck includes one's character, strength of their frith, physical strength, fate, individual will, one's abilities, and the socioeconomic conditions in which one was born.

**Wyrd and Orlæg** — The Well and the Tree (Yggdrasil and the Well of Urd) represent the cyclical nature of time and the power entombed within the cosmos. One's Orlæg was considered to be the conditions that were chosen for them before they were born, including their sexuality, gender, economic class, social class, religion, parents, country of birth, and so on. Orlæg is the stats that you start with. Wyrd, on the other hand, is the connection that you form with others, the tapestry that you weave as you interact with the world and leave your mark on it. A heathen accepts the Wyrd and Orlæg as cosmic forces and affirms the cosmological concepts they represent.

### Shamanism

Shamanism was and is still followed all over the world today. A shaman interacts with the spirit world directly via altered states of consciousness, such as vision quests and trances. The purpose of the shaman is to manipulate, guide, and utilize spiritual energy and spiritual entities in such a way that they can heal someone's illnesses, provide help to those who need it, and offer divinatory wisdom.

This ancient practice comes from the indigenous people of northern Europe and Siberia. The Proto-Germanic people considered Odin to be a master of many different disciplines, including shamanism. Shamanism has many commonalities with Norse mythology, particularly when working with spirits from the Norse pantheon.

Shamans believe that spirits exist and play a very critical role in the lives of humans. A shaman can communicate with these spirits. For example, a Nordic shaman would possess the ability to make contact with Odin's spirit and ask for aid. But not all spirits are beneficial. Some spirits can cause some serious harm, such as the djinns in Arabic lore and the draugrs in Norse mythology.

Shamanism teaches its practitioner to treat diseases caused by evil spirits.

Besides healing and working with spirits, a shaman can use trance techniques to visit other realms and enter different dimensions in search of answers. This may be done either through meditation or by consuming substances such as mushrooms.

Shamans can use familiars in the form of animals as spirit guides and message bearers. They can also perform different forms of divination, such as scrying, using runes, and throwing bones.

As a whole, this particular denomination of paganism is centered around divination and healing.

**Wicca**

Heathenry and paganism had many different forms in the pre-Christian world. Witchcraft, unlike how it is painted as an evil practice today, was a form of paganism in which the practitioners held beliefs that centered around nature, conducted naturalistic rituals, and practices that attune one to the world around them and allow them to communicate with the forces of magic that exist outside of the realm of the common folk.

Although Wicca is a revivalist, modern religion formed in the twentieth century, its roots go back in time, deriving from the wisdom of the ancient witches and warlocks who practiced the arcane art of magic. Wiccans are polytheists and can venerate any number of deities, including but not limited to gods and goddesses from the Norse pantheon.

Wiccans meet in the form of groups called covens. They don't exactly worship or venerate the biblical Satan, rather, they consider him a symbol of rebellion against the traditions put in place by Judaism and Christianity.

Wiccans channel the universal energy and perform magic with it to achieve desired effects.

The moral code of Wiccans tells them: "If it harms none, do what thy wilt."

There is no singular source from which Wiccans get their knowledge. It can be an individualistic or community-based practice based on one's preference. Like other forms of paganism, Wiccans also use rune magic, divination, scrying, and astral projection.

They also celebrate sabbaths and festivals, including Ostara and Yule.

Wiccans can choose one particular patron deity and work with them through meditation, veneration, and performing rituals.

Wicca finds its roots in Celtic paganism, but those roots are not exclusive to the Celtic. There is Germanic influence present as well, as seen in the immanent, animistic, and transcendental nature of the beliefs.

**How Do I Become a Pagan?**

Those were some of the modern versions of paganism. As a budding pagan, it is now your responsibility to treat this knowledge with the care it deserves. Throughout this book, I have given you the fundamentals of Norse Paganism and Mythology, introducing you to the various beliefs, gods, goddesses, rituals, customs, rites of passage, and stories that comprise the beliefs of Pagans the world over.

- Now, I want you to get some first-hand information by studying the Eddas and the historical accounts that are available online, reading will allow you to learn about the history, culture, mythology, folklore, and legends of Norse mythology, while giving you the freedom to decide for yourself what is true.
- Once you have perfected your theory, it is time to put it into practice. I recommend choosing a patron deity—there can be more than one—if you feel drawn to a particular one. Allow this connection to strengthen through meditation, veneration, and divination.
- You can follow the rites I've mentioned in the book or you can do your research and come across new ones. Then, if you feel inclined, you can create your rituals from the outline of pre-existing ones.
- It's best to join a community for the sake of celebrating different ceremonies, becoming a part of something larger than yourself, and performing communal rituals. But if you are more introverted, you can continue along the pagan path by yourself.

- Throughout this journey, if you come across a familiar spirit in the form of an animal, get the feeling that an ancestor is trying to get in touch with you, or simply feel the presence of an allied spirit, you should let them guide you.
- A word of warning: Some factions masquerade as Norse Pagans but are actually white supremacists and racists. You should steer clear of them at all costs. There's no connection between Norse traditions and white supremacy whatsoever.
- You should perform the rites and observe the festivals at their respective time of the year to foster a better relationship with the respective deities.
- Lastly, live your life bravely, follow the virtues embodied by the gods and goddesses, and be authentic in your everyday life. Align yourself with the beliefs that are shared in this book and Norse Paganism, and soon enough, you will become an experienced Pagan, guiding other newcomers to the light.

Sjáumst!

# LEAVE A 1-CLICK REVIEW!

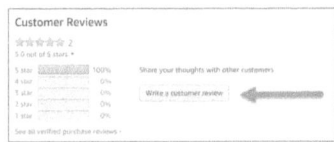

I would be incredibly thankful if you could take just 60 seconds to write a brief review on Amazon, even if it's just a few sentences!

>>Click here to leave a quick review

# CONCLUSION

It was no coincidence that you came here. Old roots run deep. Together, you and I embarked on a journey. I as your guide, you as my disciple. Whether it was the call of a god or goddess that drew you here or curiosity, you were welcome.

I wanted to share the knowledge of the old Norse religion, Norse mythology, and Norse Paganism with you to better equip you with the information you need to take a step towards being a practicing modern pagan yourself.

- I introduced you to the concept of Norse Paganism and provided you with the framework for being a Norse Pagan.
- We learned who the Norse Gods were and about the worlds that they dwelled in.
- We took a deep dive into history, uncovering the Norse timeline through the ages, including the Viking age's advent and end. But this was only the beginning.

- From there, we delved into the creation of the cosmos, learning about how the universe came into existence according to the Norse worldview. From Yggdrasil to each of the Nine Realms, we traveled through the cosmos, marveling at the grandeur of Norse cosmology.
- As it was vital for becoming a Pagan that you understood the Pagan holidays, rituals, and festivals, I shared the details of the lunar calendar with you and described the Norse holidays. We learned how the days of the week came to be known as Monday, Tuesday, Wednesday, and so on.
- In the fifth chapter, we took a deep look at the Norse Pantheon of Gods, reading their stories and learning how to venerate them.
- I showed you how rich and diverse the Norse world was, with its many creatures such as the elves, trolls, Valkyrie, and draugrs.
- We took a pensive turn and deliberated over the Norse concept of the afterlife and how the soul was divided into different pieces. We found out where the deceased went after death.
- And then our learning took a magical turn, allowing us to divine the wisdom of runes, from their origin to their meanings. We even discussed how we can use runes in our daily lives.
- I interspersed Norse mythology, Norse Paganism, and Norse history in this book in such a way that would allow you to learn both the practices and the historical significance of the practices. Similarly, we looked at the two main rites of passage— marriage, and childbirth.

- And lastly, we reviewed the various denominations of Norse Paganism that are being followed today, equipping you with the right data you need to choose the branch that suits you best.

In my eyes, you are a Pagan already. All that's left to do is put what you have learned into practice.

I sincerely wish you the best of luck on your Norse journey.

If you want to help me spread this information to more people, please leave a review on Amazon.

Thank you for reading!

# FREE GIFT JUST FOR YOU!!!

## 2023 WHEEL OF THE YEAR PLANNER

https://bit.ly/3Ux42iz

# CITATIONS AND REFERENCES

## INTRODUCTION

1. Knightly, Z. H. (2022, March 09). Introduction to Norse Heathenry. Retrieved October 15, 2022, from https://skaldskeep.com/norse/intro/

2. McCoy, D. (2019, February 08). The Ultimate Online Guide to Norse Mythology and Religion. Retrieved October 15, 2022, from https://norse-mythology.org/

3. Scott, J., Joachim, & Wright, K. (2022, November 02). A beginner's guide to norse mythology. Retrieved October 15, 2022, from https://www.lifeinnorway.net/norse-mythology/

4. Gaiman, N. (2019). *Norse mythology*. S.l.: Bloomsbury Publishing.

5. Nomads, T. (2022, March 21). Norse paganism for beginners: Quick introduction + resources. Retrieved

October 15, 2022, from https://www.timenomads.-com/norse-paganism-for-beginners/

6. Routes North. (2022, June 20). Norse paganism: What is it, and what do its followers believe? Retrieved October 15, 2022, from https://www.routesnorth.com/language-and-culture/norse-paganism/

7. Smith, R. (2019). *The way of fire and ice: The living tradition of Norse paganism.* Woodbury, MN: Llewellyn Publications.

8. The Old Nordic Religion Today. (n.d.). Retrieved October 15, 2022, from https://en.natmus.dk/historical-knowledge/denmark/prehistoric-period-until-1050-ad/the-viking-age/religion-magic-death-and-rituals/the-old-nordic-religion-today/

9. McCoy, D. (2016). *The Viking spirit: An introduction to norse mythology and religion.* North Charleston, SC: Create-Space Independent Publishing Platform.

Crawford, J. (2015). *The poetic edda: Stories of the Norse gods and heroes.* Indianapolis: Hackett Publishing Company.

## THE FRAMEWORK FOR BEING A NORSE PAGAN

1. A guide to norse gods and goddesses. (1970, October 29). Retrieved October 15, 2022, from https://www.centre-ofexcellence.com/norse-gods-goddesses/

2. Knightly, Z. H. (2021, December 29). The Norse deities. Retrieved October 15, 2022, from https://skaldskeep.com/norse/deities/

3. Heritage Daily. (2021, August 26). Yggdrasil and the 9 Norse worlds. Retrieved October 15, 2022, from https://www.heritagedaily.com/2018/08/yggdrasil-and-the-9-norse-worlds/121244

4. The nine realms in Norse mythology. (2022, July 18). Retrieved October 15, 2022, from https://skjalden.com/nine-realms-in-norse-mythology

5. Mark, J. (2022, November 01). Ten norse mythology facts you need to know. Retrieved October 15, 2022, from https://www.worldhistory.org/article/1836/ten-norse-mythology-facts-you-need-to-know/

6. Knightly, Z. H. (n.d.). Yggdrasil. Retrieved October 15, 2022, from https://skaldskeep.com/norse/yggdrasil/

7. McCoy, D. (2018, July 05). Sources. Retrieved October 15, 2022, from https://norse-mythology.org/sources/

8. Paxson, D. L. (2021). *Essential ásatrú: A modern guide to norse paganism*. New York, NY: Citadel Press Books are published by Kensington Publishing.

9. Gefnsdottir. (2013, March 19). Vanatru: Clearing up some misconceptions. Retrieved October 15, 2022, from https://adventuresinvanaheim.wordpress.com/2013/03/19/vanatru-clearing-up-some-misconceptions/

Northern tradition paganism: Northern-tradition paganism & heathenry. (n.d.). Retrieved October 15, 2022, from https://www.northernpaganism.org/general/northern-tradition-paganism-heathenry.html

## THE ORIGINS AND HISTORY OF NORSE PAGANISM

1. Nikel, D. (2022, February 03). The Viking timeline - what happened and when? Retrieved October 15, 2022, from https://www.lifeinnorway.net/viking-timeline/

2. Brownworth, L. (2014). *The sea wolves: A history of the Vikings*. United Kingdom: Crux Publishing.

3. The Viking Network. (n.d.). The Viking Timeline. Retrieved November 2, 2022, from http://www.viking.no/e/etimeline.htm

4. The National Museum Of Denmark. (n.d.). The Viking age. Retrieved October 15, 2022, from https://en.natmus.dk/historical-knowledge/denmark/prehistoric-period-until-1050-ad/the-viking-age/

5. Short, W. R. (n.d.). What happened to the Vikings? Retrieved October 15, 2022, from https://www.hurstwic.org/history/articles/society/text/what_happened.htm

6. History.com. (2009, November 04). Vikings. Retrieved October 15, 2022, from https://www.history.com/topics/exploration/vikings-history

7. Routes North. (2022, June 20). Norse paganism: What is it, and what do its followers believe? Retrieved October 15, 2022, from https://www.routesnorth.com/language-and-culture/norse-paganism

8. Nikel, D. (2020, December 03). Viking religion: From the Norse gods to Christianity. Retrieved October 15, 2022, from https://www.lifeinnorway.net/viking-religion/

9. Napoli, D. J., & Balit, C. (2017). *Treasury of Norse mythology: Stories of intrigue, trickery, love, and revenge.* Washington, D.C: National Geographic Kids.

10. Colum, P., & Pogány, W. (2019). *The children of Odin: The book of northern myths.* New York, NY: Aladdin.

## THE CREATION OF THE COSMOS

1. Creation of the world in Norse mythology. (2022, July 18). Retrieved October 15, 2022, from https://skjalden.com/creation-of-the-world-in-norse-mythology

2. Campbell-Dagnall, H. (2020, February 05). The 9 realms explained - norse cosmology. Retrieved October 15, 2022, from https://viking-styles.com/blogs/history/the-9-realms-explained-norse-cosmology

3. Ashliman, D. L. (2010, February 17). The Norse Creation Myth. Retrieved October 15, 2022, from https://sites.pitt.edu/~dash/creation.html

4. McCoy, D. (2018, July 24). The creation of the cosmos. Retrieved October 15, 2022, from https://norse-mytholo-

gy.org/tales/norse-creation-myth/

5. Greenberg, B. (2022, January 04). The Norse creation myth. Retrieved October 15, 2022, from https://mythologysource.com/norse-creation-myth/

6. Gill, N. (2018, March 03). Creation of the world in Norse mythology. Retrieved October 16, 2022, from https://www.learnreligions.com/creation-in-norse-mythology-117868

7. McCoy, D. (2018, July 28). Yggdrasil. Retrieved October 16, 2022, from https://norse-mythology.org/cosmology/yggdrasil-and-the-well-of-urd/

8. Liam. (2022, October 02). Nine realms of norse mythology (all the worlds explained). Retrieved October 16, 2022, from https://vikingr.org/norse-cosmology/nine-realms-of-norse-mythology

9. Norse cosmology. (2021, November 20). Retrieved October 16, 2022, from https://mythopedia.com/topics/norse-cosmology

10. McCoy, D. (2018, July 14). The nine worlds. Retrieved October 16, 2022, from https://norse-mythology.org/cosmology/the-nine-worlds/

## THE NORSE CALENDAR AND PAGAN HOLIDAYS

1. The Viking Calendar. (n.d.). Retrieved October 16, 2022, from http://www.vikingsofbjornstad.com/Viking_Calen-

dar.shtm

2. The Norse Wheel of the year: The Norse calendar & holidays. (2021, October 08). Retrieved October 15, 2022, from https://www.timenomads.com/the-norse-wheel-of-the-year-viking-calendar-holidays/

3. Asatru holidays. (n.d.). Retrieved October 16, 2022, from https://thetroth.org/resources/norse-pagan-holidays

4. The Viking Lunar Calendar: The names of months and days. (2022, July 18). Retrieved October 16, 2022, from https://skjalden.com/the-viking-lunar-calendar-the-names-of-months-and-days/

5. Norse holidays and festivals. (n.d.). Retrieved October 16, 2022, from http://thepaganjourney.weebly.com/norse-holidays-and-festivals.html

6. The Vikings days of the week. (n.d.). Retrieved October 16, 2022, from https://vikings.mrdonn.org/daysofthe-week.html

7. Viking festivals: A list of Scandinavian and Celtic related events. (n.d.). Retrieved October 16, 2022, from https://sonsofvikings.com/pages/viking-festivals

8. Norse Festivals. (n.d.). Retrieved October 16, 2022, from http://www.wizardrealm.com/norse/holidays.html

9. Knightly, Z. H. (2022, February 12). Norse holidays. Retrieved October 16, 2022, from https://skaldskeep.-com/norse/holidays/

10. Valkyrja - The Old Icelandic calendar. (n.d.). Retrieved October 16, 2022, from http://valkyrja.com/220915.html

## THE NORSE PANTHEON OF GODS AND GODDESSES

1. McCoy, D. (2018, September 04). The aesir gods and goddesses. Retrieved October 16, 2022, from https://norse-mythology.org/gods-and-creatures/the-aesir-gods-and-goddesses/

2. Greenberg, M., Dr. (2022, January 04). The Vanir gods and goddesses. Retrieved October 16, 2022, from https://mythologysource.com/vanir-gods-and-goddesses/

3. Friscia, M. (2021, March 29). Bragi: History and worship of the Norse god of music. Retrieved October 16, 2022, from https://www.uncoveringsound.com/bragi-history-worship-of-the-norse-god-of-music/

4. Greenberg, M., Dr. (2021, July 06). Who was Baldur in Norse mythology? Retrieved October 16, 2022, from https://mythologysource.com/baldur-norse-god/

5. Greenberg, M., Dr. (2022, January 04). Who was Frey in Norse mythology? Retrieved October 16, 2022, from https://mythologysource.com/freyr-norse-god/

6. Greenberg, M., Dr. (2021, January 18). Freya: The Norse Goddess of Beauty and Magic.Retrieved October 16, 2022, from https://mythologysource.com/freya-norse-goddess/

7. McCoy, D. (2018, July 06). Heimdall. Retrieved October 16, 2022, from https://norse-mythology.org/gods-and-creatures/the-aesir-gods-and-goddesses/heimdall/

8. Frigg – the goddess of marriage. (n.d.). Retrieved October 16, 2022, from https://historiska.se/norse-mythology/frigg-en/

9. McCoy, D. (2017, July 09). Hel (goddess). Retrieved October 16, 2022, from https://norse-mythology.org/gods-and-creatures/giants/hel/

10. Scott, J., Lagana, N., Mary, Aj, Schexnayder, S., & Crystal. (2021, October 08). Loki: The story of the trickster god. Retrieved October 17, 2022, from https://www.lifein-norway.net/loki-norse-mythology/

11. Apel, T. (2021, November 18). Njord. Retrieved October 17, 2022, from https://mythopedia.com/topics/njord

12. McCoy, D. (2018, June 30). Odin. Retrieved October 17, 2022, from https://norse-mythology.org/gods-and-creatures/the-aesir-gods-and-goddesses/odin/

13. Thor: The god of thunder: Norse mythology. (2022, July 20). Retrieved October 17, 2022, from https://skjalden.com/thor/

14. Norman. (2022, May 10). Tyr. Retrieved October 17, 2022, from https://thenorsegods.com/tyr/

15. Bragi: History and worship of the Norse god of music. (2021, March 29). Retrieved October 17, 2022, from

https://www.uncoveringsound.com/bragi-history-worship-of-the-norse-god-of-music/

## THE CREATURES OF NORSE MYTHOLOGY

1. McKay, A., Ivan, Vanoy, S., Minseo, O'Coileain, D., Draconian, . . . Bakken, T. (2021, October 08). Creatures in Norse mythology. Retrieved October 17, 2022, from https://www.lifeinnorway.net/creatures-in-norse-mythology/

2. Rhys, D. (2022, September 21). 15 unique creatures of Norse mythology. Retrieved October 17, 2022, from https://symbolsage.com/norse-mythology-creatures-list/

## THE AFTERLIFE

1. Mark, J. (2022, November 01). Norse ghosts & the afterlife. Retrieved October 17, 2022, from https://www.world-history.org/article/1290/norse-ghosts--the-afterlife/

2. The multi-part soul. (n.d.). Retrieved October 18, 2022, from https://skaldskeep.com/norse/soul/

3. McCoy, D. (2017, July 09). Death and the afterlife. Retrieved October 18, 2022, from https://norse-mythology.org/concepts/death-and-the-afterlife/

4. S., J. (2022, October 14). Norse mythology afterlife: Afterlife in norse mythology: Norse afterlife realms. Retrieved October 18, 2022, from https://blog.vkngjewelry.com/en/norse-afterlife/

5. The afterlife of norse mythology compared to the afterlife of Greek mythology. (2021, May 05). Retrieved October 18, 2022, from https://www.grin.com/document/1025978

## DIVINING RUNE WISDOM

1. McCoy, D. (2018, July 04). Runes. Retrieved October 18, 2022, from https://norse-mythology.org/runes/

2. Talisa + Sam | Two Wander. (2022, September 27). Rune meanings and how to use rune stones for divination. Retrieved October 18, 2022, from https://www.twowander.com/blog/rune-meanings-how-to-use-runestones-for-divination

3. Chamberlain, L. (2018). *Runes for beginners: A guide to reading runes in divination, rune magic, and the meaning of the elder futhark runes*. Santa Barbara, CA: Chamberlain Publications.

4. Bernott, K. (2021, March 22). The elder futhark runes and their meanings. Retrieved October 18, 2022, from http://www.shieldmaidenssanctum.com/blog/2019/3/12/the-elder-futhark-runes-and-their-meanings

5. The Pagan Grimoire. (2022, August 13). Your guide to the 24 elder futhark runes and their meanings. Retrieved October 18, 2022, from https://www.pagangrimoire.com/elder-futhark-rune-meanings/

## RITES OF PASSAGE

1. Silver, A. (1970, January 01). Rites of passage: Birth. Retrieved October 18, 2022, from http://nordicwic-can.blogspot.com/2012/12/rites-of-passage-birth.html

2. Rite of birth: The-Asatru-community. (n.d.). Retrieved October 18, 2022, from https://www.theasatrucommunity.org/rite-of-birth

3. Ruth Morales, V. (2021, August 20). A guide to Viking wedding rituals & traditions. Retrieved October 18, 2022, from https://www.yeahweddings.com/viking-wedding-traditions/

4. Harvey, S. (2021, November 08). An insight into Viking wedding and Norse wedding traditions. Retrieved October 18, 2022, from https://scandification.com/viking-wedding-and-norse-wedding-traditions/

5. Tomlin, A. (2022, October 01). All you need to know about Viking weddings. Retrieved October 18, 2022, from https://www.routesnorth.com/language-and-culture/all-you-need-to-know-about-viking-weddings/

## PRACTICING MODERN PAGANISM

1. Staff, Sigurþórsdóttir, S., Gunnarsson, O., & Helgason, M. (n.d.). 11 things to know about the present day practice of ásatrú, the ancient religion of the Vikings. Retrieved October 18, 2022, from https://icelandmag.is/article/11-things-know-about-present-day-practice-asatru-ancient-religion-vikings

2. Lafayllve, P. M. (2013). *Practical heathens guide to Asatru*. Llewellyn.

3. Ember, C. (2015, October 29). What is Vanatru? who are the Vanir? Retrieved October 18, 2022, from https://embervoices.wordpress.com/2013/10/02/what-is-vanatru-who-are-the-vanir/

4. Rokkatru for dummies - magic forums. (2015, August 11). Retrieved October 18, 2022, from https://www.spellsofmagic.com/read_post.html?post=767428

5. What is Thursatru? (n.d.). Retrieved October 19, 2022, from https://thursatru.squarespace.com/whatisthursatru

6. Odinism. (n.d.). Retrieved October 19, 2022, from https://www.compellingtruth.org/Odinism.html

7. Lokeans for dummies. (2012, October 23). Retrieved October 19, 2022, from https://www.spellsofmagic.com/coven_ritual.html?ritual=2288&coven=628

8. What is Heathenry? (n.d.). Retrieved October 19, 2022, from http://heathengods.com/what/

9. Secunda, B. (2020, May 08). What is shamanism? Retrieved October 19, 2022, from https://www.shamanism.com/what-is-shamanism

10. Berger, H. (n.d.). What is Wicca? an expert on modern witchcraft explains. Retrieved October 18, 2022, from https://www.brandeis.edu/now/2021/september/wicca-berger-conversation.html